#34-94 BK Bud
April 94

NORTH CAROLIN
STATE BOARD OF COMMUNITY
LIBRARIES
SOUTHEASTERN COMMUNITY COLLEGE

P9-DCY-191

SOUTHEASTERN COMMUNITY
COLLEGE LIBRARY
WHITEVILLE, NC 28472

HD
6279
, B47
1993

# Retiring To Your Own Business

## How You Can Launch A Satisfying, Productive, and Prosperous Second Career

Gustav Berle, PhD

SOUTHEASTERN COMMUNITY
COLLEGE LIBRARY
WHITEVILLE, NC 28472

PUMA PUBLISHING CO.
SANTA MARIA, CALIFORNIA

Copyright © 1993
by Puma Publishing Co.
Santa Maria, California
All Rights Reserved.

Library of Congress Cataloging-in-Publication Data

Berle, Gustav, 1920–
  Retiring To Your Own Business: How You Can Launch A Satisfying,
Productive, and Prosperous Second Career / Gustav Berle.
  p.  cm.
  Includes index.
  ISBN 0-940673-60-6  $14.95
  1. Retirees—Employment. 2. Self-employed. 3. New business enterprises—
Management. I. Title.
HD6279.B47  1993
658.1'141—dc20
                                                92-22196
                                                    CIP

# ABOUT THE AUTHOR

Gustav Berle has a PhD in business administration and has taught marketing and public relations courses at three universities. He has been an editor and a publisher. Since "retiring" he has accepted a two year appointment as a national director with SCORE, an agency of the Small Business Administration; has written twelve books; is teaching business ethics at Florida International University, and has no intention of ever stopping these peripatetic activities.

# ABOUT PUMA PUBLISHING

Puma Publishing is a small family run business in rural California.

We care about our customers, and are dedicated to making available, at a reasonable price, the best possible information for people starting or contemplating starting a small business.

All books sold by Puma are guaranteed unconditionally. If you're ever disappointed with our products, please drop me a line at 1670 Coral Drive, Santa Maria, California 93454.

William M. Alarid
Publisher

# ACKNOWLEGEMENT

Retirement is something you look forward to when you are working. Once you reach it, you might find that it is more mirage than miracle. Finding something useful to do is better because it replenishes the body's energy and nourishes the spirit. Making money in your retirement means that somebody out there in our world thinks that we are still worth something — and that is better still. This book is intended to show you the options and give you encouragement that it can be done, regardless of what the calendar says. The people in my life who helped me follow the path to continued performance, self-respect and even making enough money to maintain a comfortable living standard are many. A few of those that I want to thank through this literary effort are: Esther Pinto Rosenbloom, Neil and Ellen Matlins, Bert Holtje, Mike Hamilton, William Alarid, Paul F. Eiseman, John E. Daniels, Robert Williamson, Dr. John B. Bear, and the 13 million "retirees" to whom this book is addressed and who might be encouraged, as I was, to keep on going.

Gustav Berle, PhD
WASHINGTON, DC

# TABLE OF
# CONTENTS

# INTRODUCTION

A funny thing happened on the way to retirement. The plans you have been making — oh, what fun it was! — are suddenly about as valid as delivering ice cubes to the eskimos. All sorts of things have happened, most of them beyond your control. Let us count the ways:

1. Inflation has continued on its unmerry way. Even at a modest and (to quote the government spokesperson) "acceptable" level of three percent or so, the retirement home that you planned to acquire cost $50,000 when you at age thirty started your retirement planning. All of a sudden it costs $100,000 and chances are that it is considerably higher. On top of that, being older and unable to show a steady income on your mortgage application, you are required to put 30% down. There goes $30,000 plus moving and settlement costs — in cash. So, unless you are selling a home elsewhere and coming into a lump sum, you've got problems. In business that's called "cash flow."

2. Maybe one of the kids (even at thirty or forty, they're still your "kids") gets a divorce or mismanages some phase of his/her life and requires an immediate infusion of cash to keep the sheriff away, or sickness rears its ugly head. It seems to happen more often than not, and the more kids you have, the greater the mathematical probability.

i

3. Perhaps you were persuaded, some years ago, to invest in a hotshot stock that you have really not paid too much attention to during all this time — knowing that your trusty broker was taking good care of your interests. But now it is time to cash in on your savings — and lo and behold, the stock, the bank, or the company has taken a nosedive. Your nest egg, in other words, has laid an egg. Oh well, at thirty or forty, you can start all over and recoup some of the losses. But at *your* age? At *retirement* age?

---

## HOW LONG CAN YOUR SECOND CAREER LAST?

A retiree who starts a second career between age 50 and 75 has more years of active life ahead than he or she probably figured on. Government tables offer the following averages of years during which you can expect to have a productive life:

| PRESENT AGE | YEARS TO GO | |
| --- | --- | --- |
| | MALE | FEMALE |
| 50 | 25.7 | 31.2 |
| 55 | 21.6 | 26.0 |
| 60 | 17.9 | 22.6 |
| 65 | 14.6 | 18.6 |
| 70 | 11.5 | 14.9 |
| 75 | 9.0 | 11.7 |

---

4. You might have been in business for yourself, or in a partnership, and have trusted to good health, your sharp wits, the luck-o'-the-Irish, your son coming out of college to take over and pay you a couple of thousand a month, or new and as yet unknown opportunities. But none of them worked out. It happens. Unfortunately, more often than not. While we are chasing the rainbow during our peak productive years, we often neglect to keep the pot at the end in clear view.

Even if you are in reasonably good health and your mate, too, is holding up well, there are so many other ways that your planned retirement income can depreciate and be affected by unforeseen, and often uncontrollable, circumstances.

Another factor: realization of a dream. You've worked for others all your life — in a corporation, for the government, in a military career — and all of a sudden you are either at that theoretical retirement age, or you are squeezed out as the result of a corporate merger or an early-retirement enticement. But all the while that you were producing for others and receiving an assured weekly or monthly income, you dreamt of that nebulous *independence*. Some day, you promised yourself, you would go into business for yourself. YOU would be the boss and call the shots, do what you really wanted to do — perhaps turn your lifetime hobby into a paid vocation — and make scads of money.

And so here you are at the threshold of retirement and the idea of being in business for yourself stares you in the face. You've got the experience, the willingness (often called motivation), a feeling of exuberance and vigor well beyond your chronological age, the money to stake yourself in a modest business adventure, and even the tacit encouragement of your mate. (After all, it might be better than being underfoot all the time and moping about your ennui!)

This is where we come in. *RETIRING TO YOUR OWN BUSINESS: How You Can Launch a Satisfying, Productive, and Prosperous Second Career* explores the many opportunities that are available to you. It dissects the options that you now have. It shows you the many ways you can recycle your skills. But it also points in unmistakable terms to the pitfalls and potholes that can lie ahead. Always remember: your skills might be superior now, but your time is shorter. You do not have the time, and often the energy, to recoup any mistakes and losses. At this stage of your life, you have to work smarter, not harder.

Mature entrepreneurship tends to be less risky than business started during younger years. Second careers are based usually on more conservatism. That is the nature of many as they age, and it is a valid protective device. Experience is a great teacher, though not a protective device that infallibly eliminates catastrophe. Yet, with maturity and experience, and a greater degree of conservatism, reduced adventurism, more networking ability, and usually better self-financing, the Second Careerist who starts a business *after* retirement has a better than even chance to succeed once more.

While this book does not come with an iron-clad guarantee of fiscal success, it can offer a great deal of information, lead you to much introspection, show you the various options at your disposal, and point out the red flags that you need to look out for — before you decide to reduce your time on the golf course, on the scenic sightseeing highways, or on exotic cruises. And when all is said and done, a successful *second* career is every bit as satisfying as the first one. Maybe more so. It'll surprise and delight your peers that you have been so able to do it; that you have been successful at stoking your furnace even though there's snow on top.

Just make sure that you get the brain in gear before you put that latent career in motion. With *Retiring To Your Own Business* to lubricate your ambitions, it might very well be just a little smoother.

---

## WHY ACTIVE RETIREES ARE GOOD FOR AMERICA

- Working, active retirees stay healthier and thus become less of a burden to their families and the government.

- Productive retirees add to a continuing tax base instead of being a drain on it.

- Working retirees add to the nation's welfare, as well as to their own — by innovating new ideas, products and services.

- When working for others, retirement-age Americans make reliable, dependable, reasonable-cost employees.

- When becoming volunteers, retirees function effectively and economically in every domestic and international level.

G*oing*

*into business is like*

*swimming across the river.*

*You are bound to get wet.*

*Of course it also helps*

*to know how to swim.*

# FACTS AND FIGURES ABOUT RETIREMENT YOU MIGHT NOT HAVE KNOWN ABOUT

# CHAPTER I

James Michener, one of the most prolific and renowned writers of this century, marked his eighty-fourth birthday early in February of 1991. You can hardly say that he began a retirement career late in life. Michener never retired.

"The passage of time does not mean I am put out to pasture," said the grizzled author at the time. "It does make me a little tired, though. I don't feel like an elder statesman. I am working very diligently. The only change in my life is that I take a nap in the afternoon."

While he continues writing, Michener and his wife Mari enjoy the winters in St. Petersburg, Florida. He volunteers to teach writing to a small group of students at Eckerd College's Academy of Senior Professionals — combining both worlds, pursuing his famed craft as well as positive, pragmatic volunteerism. Michener's model is worth imitating.

At eighty-four, James Michener is admittedly an exception to the general demography of retirees. However, he is one of about thirty-two million Americans over sixty-five. This group is growing. At the beginning of the 20th century's final decade, they amount to 13% of this country's citizens. In another generation when today's baby boomers have reached retirement age, their category will reach an estimated 21% of the population.

More and more citizens of retirement age opt to remain at work, or, more likely, to start a new working life, either as

1

employees or as independent operators. The latter trend has
been accelerating faster than inflation. In 1960, about five or six
percent of the retirement-age population was still interested in
working. By 1985, this ambitious gray-top group had grown to
11%. As we indicated before, today it is 13% and we are heading toward 21% by decade's end.

Greater savings, greater sophistication, and greater demands
for continuing what the Italians call *la dolce vita*, the good life,
spurs retirees to continue working or at least seek second careers.

---

The Social Security Administration estimates that a retiree
wanting to live reasonably well will need the following
assured income each year, assuming a need of at least
$20,000:

| | | |
|---|---|---|
| Social Security pension | 21% | $ 4,200 |
| Investments, savings interest | 34% | 6,800 |
| Other pensions | 19% | 3,800 |
| Other benefits | 2% | 400 |
| Earned income | 24% | 4,800 |
| | 100% | $20,000 |

---

Even from this very modest (by today's standards) income
projection issued by the Social Security office, it can be seen that
unless the retiree's government payment is at least $9,000 ($750
a month), he or she needs to earn almost $100 a week from
some kind of work or business. The "investments/savings"
income referred to above also mandates that the retiree or couple have at least $85,000 invested or on deposit at eight percent,
in order to generate a before-tax income of $6,800. And all that
to have an annual income of only $20,000!

Let's consider another scenario. Financial planners, depending on their conservatism, state that retirees need from 60% to
80% of the working-life income to maintain their accustomed
living standard.

Of course there are many variables that could raise or diminish your needs. Moving into a less expensive area; living in a
mortgage-free house; enjoying good health; a windfall inheri-

tance; selling off something of considerable value; not having children who are getting into financial binds; being by nature a very pliable, well-organized person — any one or several of these factors can increase your retirement nest egg.

How does your income stack up against your assured retirement dollars? Taking the experts' figures, this is what you would be needing from all sources:

| If you are now making $25,000, you would need $15,000-$20,000 |
| If " " $30,000 " " $18,000-$24,000 |
| If " " $40,000 " " $24,000-$32,000 |
| If " " $50,000 " " $30,000-$40,000 |
| If " " $75,000 " " $45,000-$60,000 |
| If " " $100,000 " " $60,000-$80,000 |

Some of these fiscal helpmates and budget stretchers can be controlled. Many of them cannot. And since many retirees are not satisfied to go fishing or to stay home and knit little sweaters for the grandchildren, they are looking for either meaningful activities and/or meaningful additional income.

The option of developing a retirement career thus becomes more and more a desire as well as a necessity.

To start a business of one's own is increasingly one of the goals. The maturity and experience as well as money availability and diminishing needs are all ingredients in favor of that retirement career. However, there are also many pitfalls and potholes that get in the way. The number one caveat: age.

The very advantages of starting a business in one's retirement years — we have previously mentioned some and will delve into many others — also contain the seeds of caution. Because the retiree starting a new career has fewer years ahead to develop that new business, less physical capacity, occasional health limitations, and, most of all, little time to recoup any losses, it is incumbent upon him or her to eliminate as many entrepreneurial risks as possible.

New business failures are prodigious and frightening. Yet they will not hold back the true entrepreneurial spirit. And they shouldn't! However, what is needed is greater knowledge, better financing, and improved preparation. The experienced retiree embarking upon a new career has all of these, and if there are parts that are weak or lacking, now is the time to find out and make compensations. The experience and maturity of second careerists should make this more than feasible.

Some cautionary statistics are appropriate, however — like warning signs down the road that warn of sharp curves ahead.

During the first two years of a new business, an average of 35% of these businesses fail to make the third year. After five years, about 80%, or even more, of these new start-ups have gone belly-up or out of business for one reason or another.

The majority of blame is usually stated like this: "I was undercapitalized — and couldn't raise additional money." Even business writers in magazines and books echo this complaint, perhaps because it is easiest to swallow. But blaming some amorphous factor like insufficient capital does not account for the fact that thousands of businesses start and continue successfully on a literal shoestring. Obviously, money, or the alleged lack of it, cannot be blamed for all short-comings.

In reality, and in all honesty, the number one reason for business failure is management. Or the lack of it. Or the lack of knowledge, experience, imagination, judgement, ambition, education, preparation, research. Perhaps it is just as simple as waning motivation, unexpected competition, changes in methods and fashions, relocation of road patterns, usurious tax increases that could not be passed on. We will discuss these in more detail in the next chapter. But as you can already see, there are many obstacles.

The key to successful entrepreneurship, especially during these retirement career years, is the greatest possible amount of preparation. We'll tackle the various ways that you can — nay, *must* — take in order to achieve success, maximize your available cash, and optimize the additional income and satisfaction you seek in a retirement career.

## THE IMPORTANCE OF
## "SECOND CAREERISTS"

As we approach the next millennium and a greater degree of longevity, it is simply not going to be feasible to support more and more millions of retired people. Elderly citizens in the United States, totally outside productive activity, are entirely dependent on accumulated savings and Social Security payments. If they wish to assure continuity of a comfortable lifestyle, and even improve the lot of poverty level living, some sort of income-producing activity will have to be entertained by at least the more viable, more educated, more physically and mentally able members of our burgeoning population. We are not even speaking of relieving a burden upon a proportionately shrinking younger generation — the children and grandchildren who have to carry growing percentages of fiscal support for those who are old and unable to make contributions to the commonwealth.

Older Americans can be a potent and growing force, financially and socially. Already the silver-top generation accounts for half of the nation's discretionary spending and more than 75% of its wealth.

Senior households have average incomes of $25,000 or more. The figure is on the in-crease and drops off only slightly with the aging cycle. The bulk of Americans, more than half certainly, are enjoying a pretty good existence, are relatively independent, and enjoy being in charge of their own lives.

Of course, this rosy picture leaves well over 40% of retired Americans who are not in this enviable position. Some of these will of necessity be supported by the State, by relatives, or live on the bottom of the economic ladder. For many of these, a productive career program could be instituted. Examples are nanny services, hosts at social functions, teachers' aids, part-timers in retail stores, and group activities where marketable skills are pursued.

Of this approximately 40% economically deprived elderly citizens, less than 20% need financial sustenance. Economic hardships are especially acute among elderly women who lack experience beyond housekeeping.

As a matter of focused necessity, this book has to concentrate on the economically viable, better educated, and certainly the more motivated sectors of senior citizens. As a group, these Americans invest more, travel more, purchase more goods, and partake in more entertainment than at any other time in their lives.

The latter group of seniors are experienced, responsive consumers, exercising their independent options. They expect to be sold and treated with respect and intelligence. The marketplace, for those second careerists who decide to enter it again, requires competitive products and services, and people to manage it who understand the changes in our society and know how to address these changes. For those who do and are keeping up with our world, opportunities await around every turn — and age is the least of the factors to fear.

Helen T. Harris, a senior management counselor, stated it brilliantly: "Once you shift your focus from age to purchasing power, interests and lifestyles, you'll come to realize there is no risk, but unlimited opportunity."

E*ven if*

*you're on the right track,*

*you'll get run over*

*if you'll just sit there.*

—Will Rogers

# CHAPTER II

I have come across many men who completely retired. They play golf almost every day that the sun shines, and often when it doesn't. When they get tired of chasing that little ball around the greens, they go home and greet the wife, "Hey, what's for dinner?"

One couple I know is constantly on the road. He has three kids, and she has two more from a previous marriage. Altogether they have eight grandchildren, a couple of them already married. Everybody lives within a day's automobile drive; you can imagine the visiting and freeloading they do.

Fortunately, these folks are in the minority. The ones we are addressing are those who have read somewhere that retirement can kill you. One real bigtime executive was quoted in the *Wall Street Journal*, "I've had friends who ran big corporations. They went off to Florida or somewhere, and in four or five years they were dead. Their minds died first, then their bodies."

That latter statement is certainly frightening, but it is not the first time it's been bandied about, even though it might be only partially true. Still we assume, based on our experience, that vegetating is not the ideal lifestyle for most active men and women. Even the latter, who have never in their lives worked from nine to five or run a business, are better companions and happier people if they have a good reason for getting up in the morning.

Today the statisticians estimate that the average American lives nineteen years after retirement. What an opportunity for a retirement career!

9

Imagine our grandfathers who lived at the turn of the last century. By comparison, we live an average of twenty-six years longer than they did. We are in a regular longevity epidemic, and making money *after* retirement is not only a pleasure but a necessity.

Far from being hazardous to our health, retirement is a whole new ballgame. It is an opportunity to continue *living* in a style that may be different than it was before this event, but nonetheless possible — with a little planning and help.

Don't let anybody kid you that you cannot have a remunerative and satisfying lifestyle after retirement! You're not too old to start or conduct a business, to pursue a full-time volunteer position, or to take a trip around the world, if that is your choice. We're talking about business primarily — not running the 100 meter in ten seconds.

The opportunities in business, though you are of retirement age (whatever that is), are infinite. You just have to recognize your present abilities, attitudes, needs, and physical parameters. Working smarter, not harder, is the key.

---

Let's make a brief list of those assets that we have available and that we will discuss in greater detail later on:

*Preparation* — to take as much of the risk out of a new business as possible.

*Evaluation* — to ascertain our real skills.

*Research* — to learn as much as we can about our project by networking, asking questions, and using available resources such as the libraries.

*Outside Help* — to take advantage of much free assistance that is available for the asking.

---

Making money *after* retirement is usually dictated by need. The big difference at retirement age is that this need is tempered by a whole set of new factors. On the plus side are experience, lesser demands on the part of our dependent family, a greater reservoir of patience and confidence, a reputation based on past achievements, and possibly a financial base that allows us an accelerated start — or at least a choice.

On the minus side is the biggest single handicap: time. We just don't have that thirty or forty or fifty years ahead of us that allow us to experiment, explore, learn, gamble, or fail. **At our age, we must be as sure as possible.** We must put adventurism aside in favor of applying experience and even wisdom to our actions.

Appended to this chapter is a self-administered test that can help you to determine the *You Factor*. It is an entrepreneurial test that opens the window on your inner self and on your honest preparedness to go into business — especially if you have not been in business for yourself before.

This EQ Test is most difficult because it is taken by you, checked by you, and implemented by you. *You* will be the judge and jury, and the results will be your investment in irreplaceable time and money.

Since this chapter is an honest self-examination of your probable future success, let us sketch out some twenty potholes and pitfalls you need to avoid. Leaping over these obstacles is a veritable entrepreneurial survival course — and as we said above, you don't have the luxury, the *time*, to fail too many of these:

## SPECIAL PITFALLS TO AVOID AFTER RETIREMENT WHEN STARTING A BUSINESS

Dreams can be dangerous. Don't start a new business for thoroughly subjective reasons, such as:

- I want to sell something that I really like. You like books, stamps, pets, antiques, and so that's the business you want to get into. Before you do, however, find out whether such a business is really needed, how much it costs you to operate such a business, and whether you can really make money on it — unless you have oodles of big bucks and don't mind taking a chance on losing some of them.

● I want to live in Florida where it's warm.

Opening a business where you'd like to live *might* be OK, but investigate first. Do they need a business of the kind you're contemplating? Will you and your wife like it there? Is there adequate health care, transportation to visit the children, or affordable housing? Before you relocate, investigate. (And see Chapter VIII in this book!)

● I have a great idea for a new business and I'm sure I can get all the money I need from the bank.

Or, if not the bank, then the SBA. Inexperienced entrepreneurs often claim that they can start a business on a shoestring — preferably, other people's money. The truth is quite different. Money is always hard to get. See the section on how to prepare a Business Plan in this chapter to find out how to *really* do it. As you get older, it could get even harder to borrow, and more difficult to replace it if things should not prosper as quickly as you had hoped. But if your business is really needed, if you can deliver better and cheaper than somebody else, provide better quality, and have a comfortable financial cushion for yourself and your family, then go ahead. But do it correctly, whether you plan to borrow from friends, a bank, or even clients.

## 20 MORE POTHOLES AND PITFALLS

● Artherosclerotic management
● Inexperienced management
● Insufficient capitalization
● Lack of advance planning
● Insufficient cash flow
● Unrealistic advance research
● Executive burnout
● Unsupportive family
● Lousy location
● Faulty quality control

● Overloaded or lopsided inventory
● Slow turnover
● Obsolescence in products and people
● Run-away marketing
● Lazy collections
● Dipping the till
● Swiss-cheese security
● Too much "open-to-buy"
● Stalled rolling stock
● "It's tax deductible"

If you do not have answers to these pitfalls (it is only meant to be a tickler list!), then perhaps going into business on your own is not for you. However, under pain of being redundant, we shall comment on each of the above "potholes" and make sure that they are safely paved before you venture out on the limb of entrepreneurship.

*Artherosclerotic management:* leadership that is clogged up with antiquated thinking and methods. It needs roto-rooting to make it more adaptable to modern times and receptive to new-fangled ideas and concepts. Or at least open to considering innovative variations that could be more efficient and effective than the old 'tried and true' way of doing things. Maybe the old way is actually better, but give yourself a chance to look, listen, and learn — then make a judgement.

*Inexperienced management:* this is almost the reverse of the above. It is management that is still wet behind the ears, that knows everything better before even having had any pragmatic experience. It is usually the malady of the minors, but even gray-tops and silver foxes can fall victim to leadership that is more enthusiastic than experienced. Together, these two pitfalls form the most dangerous shoals on the way to entrepreneurial success and survival.

*Insufficient capitalization:* the bane of entrepreneurs. Four out of five small business planners who seek financial help from the U.S. Small Business Administration or local banks (there are nearly 300,000 of them who call the SBA each year!) ask for money. And yet an equal number of start-up entrepreneurs manage to go into business with an average of $2,000 of their own savings. Conversely, well-endowed businesses go bankrupt every day despite ample funds. But, weak management *plus* insufficient money can make for disaster. Planning for sufficient funds, having an available line of credit before starting a business or expanding, is simply smart management. Business success is spelled $uccess, especially when things don't go the way you had hoped — and most of the time they don't.

*Lack of advance planning:* since we do not have reliable crystal balls to determine what is ahead of us, we need to rely on our experience, ask those who have been there, and use research sources relating to our future business or plans. Not doing your business homework can open you to many unexpected and often unpleasant surprises — the worst of which could be bankruptcy. The latter malaise affects about 80% of all enterprises within the first five years. This being a documented fact, it is totally incomprehensible why so many businesses insist on starting and operating on a by-guess and by-gosh method. But such is human nature. Don't say, however, that we haven't warned you!

*Insufficient cash flow:* this is not the same as not having sufficient capital. It is the lack of *new* money coming in as expected, and when this lack of new money is combined with a lack of adequate cash reserves or lines of credit, then a credit crunch occurs. The next step invariably is that you cannot pay your bills, creditors start putting the squeeze on you to pay-up-or-else, and the creditors and their emissary, the sheriff, persuade you to close your doors and/or sell off remaining assets at a fraction of their worth. Planning, meticulously and honestly, how new cash will come into your business during the months ahead is one of the prime requisites of business continuity.

*Unrealistic advance research:* wishful thinking can sometimes cloud the reality of your business planning. While entrepreneurs are rightfully an optimistic lot, they need to inject a bit of caution into their research — especially new businesses, new products introduced into the marketplace, and expansions of any kind. Advance research should always include a safety cushion of a 'worst scenario'. What could happen if the best laid plans of mice and men go awry? What if projections run into absolutely uncontrollable, external circumstances? Have alternate plans and reserve cash available. Flexibility is certainly another asset of the genuine entrepreneur.

*Executive burnout:* the nature of the entrepreneur is to give 101% of his enthusiasm and energy to a task. But as Edna St. Vincent Millay once said, "...I like to burn my candle at both ends ...it gives such a bright light in the night... while it lasts." Taking occasional vacations to refresh the body and mind, varying strenuous tasks, or delegating jobs to others are just three ways to stave off the burnout that can lead to the collapse of the key person of a business — or the premature scuttling and sell-out of an otherwise successful enterprise.

*Unsupportive family:* by the time retirement age comes around, the family has usually compacted down to man and wife. The latter might think that launching a business, taking risks, endangering family security, and absenting yourself from your home rather than going on visits to the children or spending more sunset time together does not correspond to dreams of retirement tranquillity. The older 'second careerist' must make sure his mate is with him (or her) and at least morally supportive before launching into a demanding business or outside activity.

*Lousy location:* realtors have a way of dramatizing the reason for commercial business success — location, location, location. If your newly planned business, or the business you buy from somebody else, is in an inaccessible place, does not have the requisite amenities for efficient operation (traffic flow, parking, utilities, transportation, exposure, zoning, signage, et al.), keep looking for a better location. Cheap rent is not the first criterion. Rent may be only five to fifteen percent of your overhead, and the better location that could assure you more business may be but a few percentile points higher. Consider all aspects and discuss the legalities with a good lawyer before you put your name on the bottom of a costly lease.

*Faulty quality control:* as the buying public is getting to be smarter, purveyors are becoming more conscious of the need for product quality and services that perform as promised. As one writer asked, "If you don't do it right the first time, do you have the time to do it over again?" You are responsible for your products and services, as well as for the employees who represent you. Installing a quality control system in your business, selling employees on it, and monitoring it is the job of every entrepreneur who wants to survive in this highly competitive and litigious society.

*Overloaded or lopsided inventory:* An old merchant we knew a generation ago believed that a heavy inventory was like money in the bank. Unfortunately, when he died, the auctioneer sold most of his largely obsolete inventory for ten to twenty-five cents on the dollar. Inventory today becomes obsolete quicker than ever before. Constant technological, style, color, and fashion changes make it mandatory that inventory records are perpetual, turn-over of inventory increased, and buying/stocking leaner. Keeping slow-moving inventory on hand is like tying up money without interest or profit.

*Slow turnover:* most inventory of merchandise should completely "turnover" or be replaced with fresh merchandise two to five times a year. With perishable or food items, this turnover is much more frequent. Every time you turn over merchandise, you have, or should have, made a profit on it. It stands to reason that two times $1,000 is $2,000. But if you turn over goods three times instead of two times, and make $1,000 profit each time, you have earned $3,000. It's the same investment, but the returns are far greater. If you have slow turnover merchandise in your inventory, weed it out, sell it off, replace it with faster moving items. Constant inventory vigilance can make you rich.

*Obsolescence in products and people:* we mentioned earlier that technological, style, fashion, and trend changes can create obsolescence — often without your being able to do anything about it. People, too, become "obsolete" — by dying, by moving away, by outgrowing a need for your products and services as they age. This is especially true in mail order and catalog businesses. Your own "junk mail" proves the point. The successful entrepreneur is a definer of trends, is perpetually updating his knowledge of merchandise and customer needs, and checks his business records at regular intervals to eliminate costly and unproductive efforts.

*Run-away marketing:* advertising, promotion, and public relations efforts that do not or no longer serve their intended purpose. A sizable chunk of operating capital can go down the drain by ill-conceived advertisements, wrong media, unproductive size, efforts repeated because of pressure or apathy, unchecked and unresponsive ads or mailings or events. Two to ten percent of gross is often invested in such marketing efforts. Their results, too, depend on your vigilance, understanding, and skill.

*Lazy collections:* extending credit and then not paying sufficient attention to getting your money can assuredly cost you money. Doctors especially have found that if their office exerts strong efforts within the first 30 days after service to collect fees, their success rate is upward of 65%. Each month that patients are not dunned to pay, the collection rate goes down. Other businesses have found similar reactions. A lack of individual credit collections has led to the spectacular rise of credit card systems. Despite the two to six percent charged by the latter to businesses that use them, this collection fee usually turns out to be cheaper than the businesses' own collection efforts.

*Dipping the till:* this is self-applied larceny. The entrepreneur takes money out of the cash register for lunch, for going out, for paying for personal items. Cash income is especially vulnerable to till-dipping. After all, nobody will know and no taxes have to be paid on such income. If it remains minor, nobody will be the wiser. But if the business owner takes too much money out of the register, and reports too high inventory losses ("shrinkage" as they like to call it!), the IRS can catch on right quickly. Still, we have known retailers who always have several hundred dollars of "walking around money" in their pockets, which is never mentioned — until they plan to sell their business.

*Swiss-cheese security:* a term for security that is full of holes and loopholes. Regrettably, most thievery comes from within, not from outside intrusion. Shoplifting, too, is a scourge in some areas and even has threatened businesses with bankruptcy. Of course, many a clever bookkeeper has absconded with company money, especially in these days of electronic cash transfers. The entrepreneur must be just a little smarter, know every nook and cranny, every method and devious possibility by which goods can be removed from his premises without payment, and in all cases where employees handle cash or precious commodities, protect himself with bonding that employee. If a bonding company refuses to insure an employee for a sound reason, do not hire that person.

*Too much 'open-to-buy':* sometimes having too much capital becomes a temptation to buy more than can rationally be sold. Even in a service business, some entrepreneurs do not know how much to charge in relation to the time they devote to service — and service time, like merchandise, has a very specific value that must be cost-accounted and charged out. The term comes from department stores who give each departmental buyer a certain amount of money (open-to-buy) with which to acquire merchandise for that season or period or event.

*Stalled rolling stock:* trucks and cars and other vehicles used by a business that are not utilized efficiently, either by not being adequately maintained or by being idle. Considering that a delivery vehicle can cost $1,000 a month or more, not utilizing it to perform its intended function is a costly waste in depreciation, maintenance, insurance, and sometimes manpower.

*"It's tax deductible":* excusing a purchase or acquisition because, after all, it is a legitimate tax-deductible item. This is spurious and foolish reasoning. If a business pays any taxes at all, such expenditures are still coming mostly out of the entrepreneur's pocket. Expenses for travel, entertainment, gifts, and so-called business acquisitions are primary temptations. Be advised that though these are in effect tax-deductible on income tax reports, the IRS is becoming more critical of these types of expenditures. If you make them, be sure to document them with receipts and reasons.

## THE E.Q. (ENTREPRENEURIAL QUOTIENT) TEST

Over the years, psychologists have found that certain characteristics displayed by successful business men and women are fairly common. Some of these can be acquired or learned; others are built in. We grow up with the latter and can do little about acquiring them beyond being cognizant of them. If, for instance, you are a third generation Yankee, you cannot be the scion of an immigrant family. You cannot change your pre-adolescent behavior, but you can realize and perhaps compensate for it by knowing that certain actions while growing up will now help you to become a successful entrepreneur. Here is a typical, brief test that will take just a few minutes to complete. Make your own analysis once you have completed it. It will help you spot your assets and debits. Of course by this time, having arrived at or near normal "retirement age", changing your personality is quite impossible. Still, being forearmed is being forewarned. Experience and wisdom are on your side; time is not. Ready? Let's go...

## E.Q. TEST

1. Are you basically an optimist?

2. Entrepreneurial personalities are usually the restless types, easily bored with repetitive tasks. Are you?

3. Uniquely, many people in business for themselves are the children of immigrants. Are you?

4. Most entrepreneurs are not known for their brilliant academic achievement. Quite to the contrary — many of them were average students. Where do you stand?

5. Being self-contained and self-sufficient in high school and college, rather than a social butterfly and a joiner, are trademarks of many entrepreneurs. What were you?

6. Even before high school, would-be entrepreneurs were self-sufficient loners. Do you recall your attitudes?

7. When you were in junior and senior high school, did you ever work after school? Sell things? Have a newspaper route? Or babysit? Entrepreneurial bend shows up early.

8. Young children who displayed stubbornness and independence in the early, formative years usually made better entrepreneurs when they grew to maturity. Do you remember how you were back when?

9. Money-handling skills, which entrepreneurs must have, are shown early on — even in junior and senior high school and college. Were you a good adolescent money manager?

10. Making notes and writing down tasks to do, names to remember, ideas to develop — these are all traits that foretell an entrepreneurial, creative spirit. Do you do that? Have you done that?

11. If you go into a new area, do you study a map or get directions in advance? If you vacation, do you study the destination in advance? When you go shopping, do you make comparisons or read up on Consumer Reports? Entrepreneurs are risk takers, but they minimize risks by being informed ahead of time. Do you?

12. Are you a follower or a leader? Do you often take new and different paths from the rest of the crowd? Entrepreneurs often prefer to strike out on their own instead of joining the flock. How do you feel about that?

13. Being in a rut or performing repetitive, daily routines is boring for most entrepreneurs, and often the cause of their contemplating a business of their own. How did you decide to go into business?

14. Entrepreneurship is basically risky. If you were a bank loan officer or other type of lender, do you think that lending money *to you* is OK?

15. In the worst-case scenario, your new business failed. Would you literally get up, dust yourself off, and start all over again?

16. Starting a business, even buying another's business, means lots of hard work, long hours, and personal sacrifices. Are you up to such demands?

17. Let's say you've gotten your current project successfully off the ground. Would you start another one?

18. You've got a total of $10,000 in the bank and you want to start or buy a new business. Would you risk most or the major part of your own money?

19. Needing more money, would you make up a business plan or financial proposal and try to persuade others to lend you additional money?

20. Starting up a new business, you have a dozen simply great ideas. Which one to pursue? Would you ask around? Do some networking? Conduct a market research study? Read up on books and trade journals in the library?

Obviously, all these questions and statements should be answered positively, or as positively as possible — as long as you answer them honestly. After all, the only person you will be fooling by cheating will be yourself. If most of the answers are positive, go ahead and enjoy!

## THE MONEY MYTH

Operating capital, the money you have on hand to operate your business, pay your immediate bills, and pay for your own personal needs, and cash flow, the money that will be coming in from the sale of products and performing of services, combine to make some unusual images.

As we indicated previously, most people going into business — and that means about 80% to 85% percent of them, according to inquiries fielded by the SBA hot line Answer Desk — put money as the number one requirement for entering the business world on their own. Innumerable books and magazine articles do little to dispel this myth, and a myth it is.

The number one need in going into a business of your own is management. Money indubitably comes next. The proof is that many businesses, especially financial institutions loaded with millions of dollars, go broke — despite healthy capitalization and even ample cash flow.

What happens in the latter cases is that they spend more money than they have to compensate for these expenditures. They rack up bills higher than the cash that is coming in during this period. They make questionable investments, lured by promised high returns, and later find that the high profits vanish along with their capital investments.

What is needed then is a totally honest and realistic projection of what money can be expected to come in without fail. There is no sense in being too optimistic about making up a cash flow statement, because you will be the only one fooled by your overly generous estimates. To err on the side of conservatism is being pragmatic.

To prepare a cash flow statement for yourself, to see how much money you really need to run a business, or how much might realistically be generated by a business you plan to purchase, use these seven criteria:

1. *Balance sheet:* this form shows the profit and loss of a business over a period of time. If it is a projected business, you will not, of course, have these figures. You can, however, make some sound projections if you know the business. Ask a non-competing friend about his or her experience in a similar business, or check with a trade association or knowledgeable accountant about profit and loss under varying conditions. If you are planning to buy a closely held or personal business, the recorded cash flow needs to be scrutinized closely, as in such a business some cash income and fringe benefits are not always reflected in the balance sheet.

2. *Owner's salary:* you need to take into consideration your own continuing needs or, if contemplating the purchase of another's business, the real income of the previous owner.

3. *Benefits:* in a small enterprise, many benefits must be considered and accounted for. These might include insurance on your person or key-man insurance, a car, a savings plan, allowances for travel and entertainment, health protection, and anything else that can stand the scrutiny of a tax examiner.

4. *Interest:* if you plan to borrow money from investors, family member, a financial institution, or even from yourself, you need to project repayments and interest on the balance. The more you borrow the more you have to pay back and the higher your interest factor. It is wise to consider this carefully, as there is no need to borrow more than you need and be saddled with an injuriously high payback schedule.

5. *Nonrecurring expenses:* in the initial stages of a business, numerous expenses will occur that are one-time costs. You might need a computer, some software, a typewriter, telephone installation, basic office supplies, a vehicle, business stationery, and tooling-up costs for an accountant or attorney, announcements, and a sign. Advance cash flow projections must account for these, even if they can be amortized over several subsequent months. In this projection, consider leasing of equipment and rolling stock as an option to cash outlays.

6. *Noncash expenses:* depreciation is an expense that must be taken into consideration as it applies to property, equipment, and inventory of goods. At the end of the forecast period, such items will be reduced in value and be carried on the books at diminishing values. This entry is necessary to achieve a valid projection of your assets.

7. *Equipment and supply replacement:* during the period of your current cash flow projection, if some equipment needs to be replaced or supplies need to be repurchased or added, you need to account for such expense in your cash flow table. If you are postponing some structural additions, for instance, hoping to do so later in the period, this projected cost has to be accounted for as well.

A cash flow projection should also take into consideration one very important and likely item: unforeseen expenses. Few entrepreneurs have an unfailing crystal ball. Financial consultants will invariably advise that ten to twenty-five percent be set aside for unforeseen, unaccountable, or overlooked miscellany. Such caution is especially appropriate when planning to float a loan.

## TEN DECISION-HELPERS TO DEFEAT DISAPPOINTMENT

Making that big leap into entrepreneurship is fraught with much doubt. There can be pitfalls or there can be stepping stones to success. Here are a few points to consider:

1. After the initial enthusiasm and euphoria, can you honestly say that you have the skills and knowledge that others will spend money to buy?

2. Since *you* are the principal product in your new business, consider: how well known are you in that field? Have you done any networking? How active are you, or are you planning to be, in trade and professional groups?

3. If you are very lucky, you might have some sales, contacts, or even contracts lined up before you start your retirement business. If not, it might take months for that first customer

or client to develop. Have you provided sufficient resources to tide you over until your financial needs are met?

4. Does your experience and market research indicate where your business is going to come from?

5. Increase your own visibility before and during your start-up. Attend meetings; try to give talks before pertinent groups; send in articles to related trade journals.

6. Do you have the requisite enthusiasm and confidence for the launching of a new business? Such attitudes are infectious and will attract people and business to you.

7. Do you belong to or plan to join a professional or trade group in your field? Plan to attend meetings, conventions, seminars, and peruse their trade journals and newsletters — even going back for a year — to learn what's new in your field.

8. Check the library and book stores for literature on your business. Much can be learned from the printed pages written by experts or researchers in your business.

9. Keep a tight rein on your cash. Overhead can easily get away from you when you have a sizable lump sum available in your new business bank account.

10. Charging the right amount for your services (which is more difficult than pricing products) is vital to your business' well-being. Take into consideration *all* of your overhead expenses, including travel time, research, administrative costs, and office overhead (even if this is a home-based business).

In the next chapter we will discuss ways and means of getting help from outside sources — usually free or at very low cost.

## RECESSION-PROOFING YOURSELF
## HOW TO STAY AT THE TOP
## WHEN THE BOTTOM FALLS OUT!

When retirement approaches or you are already retired, a dozen scenarios can come up — usually quite unexpectedly — that impact your wealth negatively. This is not a scare tactic, but just an application of common sense.

None of these possibilities need to happen — but they just might. We want to enumerate some of them so that you can be aware of the many ways that your personal finances, and those of any enterprise you might want to start or have already begun, can be influenced. Many of them are beyond your control. Some of them are of national and even international scope. Still, if you are prepared with knowledge, you can hedge. You can divest yourself of some losers and emphasize the winners, and you can prepare yourself by increasing your cash position.

The negative possibilities to which all of us, especially retirees and near-retirees, are exposed include:

- Business bankruptcy, sometimes brought on by circumstances beyond your personal control

- You are fired from your job or the job is simply eliminated for economic, technological, or personal reasons.

- Corporate merger squeeze-out

- Early retirement, voluntary or not

- Unforeseen sickness or accident

- Family member gets in trouble, forcing you to quit.

- Natural disaster strikes.

- Man-made disasters, such as strikes, environmental problems, etc.

- Economic recession, local or national

- Product and style changes as a consequence of technological, social, or international changes beyond your control

- Uncontrollable local changes, such as injurious tax increases, changes in road patterns, traffic re-routing, et al.

- Unbeatable competition moves into your market.

There are a dozen possibilities in this scenario. Can you think of other pitfalls against which you need to guard?

## DOWNTURN ANTIDOTES

There are a few steps you can take in good times or bad to stave off possible problems or put yourself in a more secure position, especially fiscally, should an unexpected problem hit you over the head. Here are a few "safety helmets":

- Who owes you money? Get more aggressive about collecting. Don't let any debt mount up past 45 days, if you can help it.

- Extend payments. Maintain a business checking account that pays interest, no matter how little. Then pay promptly, but at the end of the payment period. Example: If you get a bill on the fifth of the month, you have usually 30 days to pay it, unless a two percent net 30 discount is built into it. If not, pay the bill on the fifth of the following month and collect interest on the full amount. If the bill is for $1,000 and you get five percent per annum from the bank, you are earning $50÷12=$4.16 on your money.

- Make expenditures only for the "must have" items. Example: A magazine for $3.00, lunch out for $7.50, taking the car downtown costing one gallon in gas ($1.20) plus parking ($6.50) costs $18.20 for the day.

  You can take a magazine along from home or buy a newspaper, brown-bag your lunch, and car pool. Conceivably, you can save $15 a day or $75 a week.

- Inventory control. Merchandise that does not turn over as quickly as it should or even becomes obsolete on the shelf, loses money faster than inflation. Institute better controls and get rid of the slow-moving inventory. Cash tied up in unproductive "assets" is losing money.

- Cash flow projection. Determine a realistic and honest budget for yourself as well as for your business; determine what you need to spend and what you want to spend during the next period. This applies to all size businesses and to every individual. If you know pretty accurately what money you have coming in (and, please, no wishful thinking!), then you will know what expenditures you can make for personal purposes, for additional inventory, or for capital acquisitions.

- Do you really need it? If you need merchandise, supplies, furnishings, machinery, promotional/marketing investments — is it really necessary at this time? Is it balanced by corresponding income as a result of that acquisition? Look at it like an IRS examiner might — the expenditure is deductible *if* it generates an income.

- Impulsive actions always are costly. Think twice about your personal and business actions. A little forethought invariably increases efficiency, saves money, and prevents "Excedrin headaches."

- Your nose knows. Don't cut it off to spite your face. Partners, employees, suppliers, landlords, bureaucrats, auto mechanics, telephone operators, and even the spouse can get under your skin and ruin your day. Invariably this impacts your business. Count to ten, go out for a walk, "take five" to read the paper — do whatever is necessary to get back on an even, calm keel. You know what works best for you.

## BUYING SOMEBODY ELSE'S BUSINESS: HEADACHE OR SHORTCUT?

Retirement often is not retiring *from* something but *to* something. Some men and women just cannot stand the lassitude of an undirected life. They need to *do* something. Even those who had a business and sold it start thinking about the good aspects of their past entrepreneurial existence — and think they can do it all over again, only better.

Other retirees have never been in business before, but they have always had the dream of doing things *their* way, having the relative freedom of decision that comes with business ownership, and hopefully make lots of money, especially *cash* money.

So you start perusing the Business Opportunities columns in the Sunday newspaper and having a business broker show you around the various available businesses-for-sale. There are some pitfalls and potholes in owning a business, some of them were covered earlier in this chapter and in the long list of questions in the prior section on franchising.

The two salient factors to consider, once more, are these: (1) Your own aptitude for the kind of business you want to buy, as well as your financial liquidity; of course, and (2) the reasons, the real, honest reasons, why this business is for sale.

Make yourself a checklist of questions to ask, or to have in your mind, before you even answer an ad, venture forth with a broker, or waste any time looking at existing businesses for sale. One of the soundest sets of questions is the one a banker or money lender might ask when you approach him for a loan on that business. Mind you, at this stage, when you are only looking and analyzing, you need not get hard answers or evidence on all of these points — but it is nonetheless good to know what might be in the financial officer's mind, just in case you need to ask one for a business loan.

## *BUYING-A-BUSINESS CHECKLIST*

- When was the business started and by whom?

- What are the real reasons this business is for sale?

- How much is the asking price and how was this determined?

- Is there an appraisal by a licensed appraiser?

- How much of the total asking price is for good will?

- Will the seller take back a note for any balance and if so, for how much?

- How do sales compare at the present time with sales for the past two previous years?

- If there has been a decline, what reasons are given for this?

- How can you, under your management, reverse the decline?

- What does the asking price include (inventory, fixtures, equipment, property, good will, accounts receivable)?

- Who are the creditors who have sold goods or services to the present owner?

- What were the terms under which the above were sold?

- What is the value and age of current inventory?

- What are the amounts and ages of accounts receivable?

- What capital assets are included, if not already explained in No. 10? Condition?

- Who is responsible for the debts of the business and what are they?

- Are there appraisals for the above assets?

- Has there been any advertising or promotion of the business, what kind, and what estimated impact has been achieved?

- Are there any patents or trademarks that are included in the sale?

- Are there any licenses, permits, or franchise agreements?

- What kind of a lease is in force (length, amount)?

- If land is involved, is there a valid deed?

- If any portion of the property is under construction, what contracts are in existence? How much still needs to be completed?

- Are there any management contracts with employees who remain with the business?

- Is there any insurance in force with remaining employees?

- What maintenance contracts are in existence?

- What credit cards are being used; under what agreements?

- Have any annual statements or reports been issued in the past?

- Who are the major customers/clients? Length of time doing business with the company? Amount of business done? Credit standing?

- Are there any other legal documents pertinent to the future operation of the business? Waivers? Agreements?

After all is said and done, the site has been checked, traffic counted, all the lawyer's and accountant's questions answered, financial questions satisfied — there still remains the key to it all: YOU. Can you handle this business? Is this a business you can really handle at this point in time? If you can still answer in the affirmative, then go ahead.

If you are set on or exploring the possibilities of buying somebody else's business, there are some basics to keep in mind — even if you are a lifetime entrepreneur or have been an executive with a large corporation. Ask first: Why is the seller trying to sell his or her business? Are you truly qualified to run this kind of business? Does buying a business, any business, jeopardize your personal assets or family relationships? Is the business losing money, or is the economy or that particular industry in a serious slump? If any of the answers make your buying-a-business efforts dubious, better hold off a decision at this time. Or, study this questionnaire to see whether you are really on the right track. Always remember that at "retirement age" you will have less time and less opportunity to recoup any losses. Once again, let's take an honest look:

- Buying another's business will reduce some risks and save time, but should you take on another business's problems or start a business of your own?

- What kind of business do you want to buy? Are you really capable of running that kind of business?

- Is the seller willing to take back some of the debt? Or will he help you finance the purchase price through a financial institution?

- Does the seller have a business plan that you can study? Will it be helpful to your efforts to get outside financing?

- Have you talked to non-competing business people who know the seller and his business? A banker, current lender, suppliers, Better Business Bureau, chamber of commerce, or credit bureau?

- If the business location is important, have you checked traffic, signage, parking, transportation, zoning, and insurance?

- Here's a personal question: If you are married, how does your spouse feel about your plans? Will this business fit into your accustomed or planned lifestyle?

- Are the terms of sale comfortable? Does the up-front payment leave you enough cash to operate safely?

- Are you inheriting present management? What are the commitments to such employees? Contracts? Insurance? Benefits? Bonding?

- What kind of a lease exists? Is it assignable? Renewable? At what terms?

- Are any repairs or improvements necessary that might impact your present cash availability?

- Do you have a list of reliable suppliers? Are there any written or unwritten agreements?

- Is there inventory that goes with the deal? In what condition is it and has it been verified as to quantity, age, value?

- Are you buying accounts receivable? Accounts payable? On what terms and within what time frame?

- If the business includes real estate, do you have an appraisal of both condition and value? Is there any lien against it? If the seller retains it, can you have an option for future purchase?

- A seller might regard his business as his baby. Will he remain with it until you can be comfortable with it by yourself? Will he be available to give advice or assistance and for how long?

- Do you have a non-compete clause with the seller? Has this been scrutinized by your lawyer?

- If you are working with a broker, who is paying his 12% (on an average) fee? Is he getting you the best deal? After all, the higher the purchase price, the greater his brokerage fee.

- Have you checked out current or potential competitors? You can ask Dun & Bradstreet Information Services (for a price) for custom-made business profiles.

- Are you competent to analyze the business's legal and accounting records? If you are not 100% certain, do you have competent counsel to do this for you?

As a final caveat: Don't let your enthusiasm and anxiety get in the way of a good deal. Impatience can cost you dearly. Be a little skeptical, inquisitive, and diligent. A few thousand dollars invested before the purchase, for a professional appraisal, can save you tens of thousands later.

## IF YOU PLAN TO HIRE EMPLOYEES, OR DEAL WITH THE PUBLIC, PRACTICE
## E N T I C E

ENTICE stands for Ethics, Niceties, Trust, Influence, Consistency, Equity. Here is what they mean:

*Ethics* stands for integrity. A good boss or manager sticks to it. He honors agreements; refuses to take unfair advantage of customer or employee, even down to such personal behavior as returning phone calls and being on time for appointments.

*Niceties* is an extension of ethics. Being nice to people, whether they work for you or deal with you, is simply the right thing to do. Honey always catches more flies than vinegar. Our grandparents already said that.

*Trust* is the extent to which others believe what you tell them. It is also called credibility. If you make a promise, stick to it and deliver. Nothing will improve business more than to have others trust you; nothing will destroy it more quickly than when public and employee trust in you stops.

*Influence* can increase your worth. Make sure that authority goes along with responsibility; that those who have a stake in your business also have a say.

*Consistency* of performance and quality applies both to managerial action and to product and service delivery. It removes doubt from others minds, whether they are on your payroll or buy from you.

*Equity* means fair and equal distribution of rewards and sanctions for similar performances.

And if there is one more letter to be added to ENTICE, add an 'S' that stands for "Suggestion Box". This is a simple device that allows those you work for and those who work with you to express themselves in confidence and privacy. If a reward system is attached to this communications device, some valuable contributions can be obtained and explosive problems may be defused. Remember that each of these devices...ENTICES.

## AN OFFICE AT HOME: PROS AND CONS

Of the 700,000 incorporated businesses, 500,000 sole proprietorships, and 100,000 partnerships launched in an average year, a growing number are (1) started by retirees, and (2) operated out of homes. There are many advantages, of course, not the least of them being the ease of going into business without setting up a formal office elsewhere, and the substantial savings in both tooling-up expenses and tax deductions. However, there are many drawbacks which have to be considered and for which compensating alternatives have to be designed.

Probably half of the at-home businesses started by retirees are as consultants in the very fields from which they retired. The advent of the computer, facsimile, and more sophisticated telephone equipment has made this both feasible and operationally time- and money-conserving. Since most actual business contacts are made away from the home office, that is, in the customer's or client's business location, working at home is not so bad after all — as long as some basic ground rules are observed:

1. Make sure your working place is private and functional, devoid of distractions of home life.

2. Install your own telephone and answering equipment.

3. Get good tools — typewriter, computer, fax — that enable you to operate professionally. An adequate desk, chair, lamps are vital.

4. Produce professional evidence to the outside world — good business stationery.

5. Maintain rigid discipline for yourself — reasonable hours of work, filing, correspondence, telephone calls, good records.

6. Be serious about your business by eliminating "buttinskies" who waste your time on the phone or with visits during working hours.

7. Don't cocoon yourself just because you work at home. Make appointments with clients; even go to the library. Go out to lunch occasionally.

8. Avoid piles (papers, publications, pendings) and eliminate "clutteritis." It is too easy to get messy and inefficient when working at home in limited space.

A word about taxes. It is too easy to hide behind the anonymity of a home office. The IRS, however, because of the tremendous growth of home-based businesses, has become very attentive to this category of enterprise. Form 8829 has to be filed along with Schedule C, however, proper use of this form will cut down on audits.

Form 8829 can actually be a boon. It takes you through all possible tax deductions: rent, household utilities, fix-up costs, mortgage interest, property taxes, insurance, and equipment. This "walk-through" might save you money, as long as it is honest and rational.

## FRANCHISES: EASY TO BUY, EASY TO FINANCE, BUT ARE THEY FOR YOU?

When an entrepreneur of retirement age is thinking of going into his or her own business, the most important ingredient to consider is *time*. Obviously, at fifty or sixty or older, you have less time to develop the enterprise. Even with superior skills and wide experience, launching a brand new business takes time to set up and develop a customer base, iron out the inevitable wrinkles, and establish a comfortable *modus operandus*.

Now, if a new business already had an established pattern, was easier to finance, and had a good record of survival, would that not be attractive?

The answer to the above is a good franchise.

The more than half a million franchises in this country generate nearly two-thirds of a trillion dollars. About 35% of all retail sales in the U.S. stem from franchise operations and by the end of this decade, it is estimated that one-half of all retail business will be conducted by franchisees. Since a franchised business has theoretically been tried and proven by the franchisor, it offers the retiree a short-cut to success.

Then what are the cautions?

First of all, consider your own situation. Buying a franchise means buying an obligation. You invest a considerable amount of dollars up front. You contract and promise to devote your best, full-time efforts to make the franchise succeed (after all, you are obligated to pay a percentage of your gross to the franchisor, in the majority of cases), and you have invested precious savings in a franchise fee and equipment. There is another caution: The International Franchise Association surveyed 192 small franchises and found that 21% were either bankrupt or had financial problems. All of these and other marginal ones — even big ones such as Diet Centers — have run into franchisee resistance when they did not or could not deliver the post-agreement support they had promised.

One good thing about looking at franchise opportunities is that you don't have to look very far. Franchise trade shows are held all over the map. If you keep a tight grip on your checkbook, you can visit numerous franchise shows, talk to their glib reps, then visit operating franchisees in non-competitive areas and make your decision. An annual franchise handbook is published ($35) by Info Franchise News, PO Box 550, Lewiston, NY 14092. The IFA itself publishes an annual directory of its 600-plus members with complete details; 250 pages for $6.95. Numerous other sources are available at your library, such as Dow-Jones-Irwin, *Entrepreneur* magazine, and Pilot Books. The SBA, too, has a special desk to handle franchise matters.

Even though a Franchise Offering Statement is required by law, some basic precautions should be taken if you plan to go the franchise route of entrepreneurship. Here is a list of possible questions that you will want to take along or ask a potential franchisor — after you have determined that (1) you are interested in that particular franchise, and (2) that the up-front money required by the franchisor is within your pocketbook range:

## FRANCHISEE QUESTIONNAIRE

1. Would *you* be satisfied with a franchise that sets up business rules and parameters not necessarily your own?

2. Do you have the required temperament and skills to run this type of franchise business?

3. Candidly now — is there any other way you can operate this type of business without buying a franchise?

4. Are you sufficiently capitalized — your own and possibly borrowed capital — to pay for the going-in costs as well as first-year operating costs, plus a little cushion in case things don't go as rosily as you (and the franchisor) paint it?

5. If you are buying this franchise from an existing franchisee, why is the latter selling it in the first place?

6. Will the franchisor give you some existing franchisees' addresses and operating data so that you can check them out?

7. What are you actually buying with your franchise fee?

8. How much pre-opening training are you getting?

9. How much post-opening training, supervision, and guidance can you expect, per your contract?

10. How much material must you buy from the franchisor in the future and for how long?

11. Will the franchisor take up any opening expenses — such as property, signs, equipment, basic inventory?

12. Again, if you are taking over an existing franchise business, is this a highly personal one, or can somebody else get into it with a fair chance of success?

13. If this is an existing franchise, would it be possible to buy a share in it and work in it for a while, with an option to buy the balance at some future time?

14. What kind of a lease is available, if outside space is needed?

15. Is this a cash business or is everything charged or billed?

16. How close are the same franchises located to your potential location? And what territorial protection do you have?

17. Do you have any information on the future trend of this particular type of business?

## FINANCIAL PREPAREDNESS

It may appear that we have minimized the importance of money in launching a business. Certainly it is important, but it does take second place behind management.

Still, having a clear picture of your financial needs is vital — perhaps even more so at this age. As we get older, our physical vigor tends to decline and unexpected needs can arise with greater frequency; but the time to recoup losses is shrinking steadily. We cannot make as many mistakes — if any    — as we might have allowed ourselves during our younger years.

For all these reasons, we need to put our experience and intelligence to work and do a pragmatic Net Worth Statement and Cash Flow Assessment or Projection. This necessary task should be part of a more comprehensive Business Plan (which is described in detail in this chapter). It is likely that the completion of these twin tables will show us that (1) we do not have enough money to comfortably engage in the enterprise of our dreams, or (2) that we do not need as much as we had estimated.

In the first case, we need to pare down the business we might be envisioning, or be satisfied with a smaller share of the pot — taking in a partner or allowing others to have a portion of the business through investment in it and sharing in its possible profits. In the second case, and this happens quite frequently, astute management, experience, and patience, combined with careful planning, can often reduce the need for vulnerable capital. The average small service business can be started for $1,500 to $2,000 as long as it is operated on a cash basis. Perhaps it can be operated out of one's home with a minimum of pomp and circumstance.

Let's start now with a credible and realistic financial estimate. The first draft is for your eyes only, so there is no sense in fooling yourself. If you do go for outside financing, you will indubitably need to look at it from the point of view of the financial officer. The Cash Flow Projection, however, is advisedly a more conservative table. It must accurately reflect your true — even conservative — estimate of what your business can provide in real income. To overestimate is to jeopardize the collateral that you will probably have to put up — and at retirement age, this could be disastrous.

## HOME-MADE MONEY:
## BORROWING FROM YOURSELF

Your home is your cash box. If you have been paying a mortgage for decades, chances are that the homestead is either paid up — leaving only taxes, maintenance, and insurance as the sole shelter expense — or has built up considerable equity.

Banks and savings-and-loans have made it seemingly easy to cash in on this home equity, usually fattened well beyond its initial purchase price by inflation. Equity borrowing, reverse mortgages — the latter sometimes called an equity conversion loan — or simply refinancing are some of the options to obtain working capital for a retirement business.

Of course, there is also the simple sale, providing the old home can be sold at a reasonable price in this vacillating real estate market. The latter is usually a poor method of raising funds, because despite its inflated value, the new homestead — whether another home or new condominium — can cost as much or more than the current upkeep of the old home.

But then there is renting. If the old home is sold at a favorable price and the next shelter becomes a rental accommodation, then considerable cash can be generated for a business. This method has psychological implications that not all elderly persons can absorb. Women, especially, tend to hold on to their nest. To remove them from their accustomed home and roots is often traumatic and even destructive. It takes an emotionally strong person, a viable alternative, and considerable family support to uproot many elderly from their accustomed milieu — even if such a move involves a change from a deteriorating and aging Northern suburb to a sunny, palm-studded new condominium in Florida, Southern California, or Arizona.

If no other financing methods are available for a new and fairly foolproof retirement business, the reverse mortgage may make sense to an elderly entrepreneur. Here is how it works.

The reverse mortgage allows a home owner to borrow small amounts of money on the appraised value of his home each month. It allows the debt to accrue with no repayment necessary until the owner's death. At that time, the house is sold at the current market value and the loan, plus interest and expenses, is repaid to the lending institution. It sounds all very simple, but in its real-life application, it can be much more complicated.

For example, the amount of money the lender pays the home owner depends on both the appraised value of the property and on the age (i.e., longevity) of the seller. A sixty-five year-old man with a life expectancy of eighty, let's say, can expect 15x12 monthly payments or 180 monthly installments. If the house was appraised at $180,000, that should generate approximately $1,000 a month in capital.

If the owner beats the odds of the life expectancy table, and payments total more than the home's value, the lender usually suffers the loss. In some cases, however, payments stop when the collateral, the home's appraised value, has reached its maximum.

Reverse mortgages can be set up for life or for a fixed term, like five years, which might be the outside number of years it should take for a new business to become profitable or be relinquished. The "loan" can also be structured as a line of credit to be drawn as needed or as a lump sum payment. Such payments from the lender are not subject to income tax or Social Security income ceilings.

The major drawbacks of reverse mortgages are that good terms are often hard to find; the heirs are deprived of any residue. This might create strains in the familial relationship; some lenders insist on sharing in any future appreciation of the property since they too are taking certain risks. Up-front fees and interest rates can be quite steep, especially if you retire again or sell the business and thus cancel the long-term loan. Finally, if you are not in your sixties or seventies but only in your fifties, the monthly proceeds can be too small to be helpful. Then, too, you must make sure that, if you live long enough, no clause forces you to move out of your home before you are ready or have alternate living facilities available.

Two additional caveats to watch for are clauses that cancel the loan if the owner fails to maintain the property in accordance with the lender's contract or becomes too elderly to remain in the home and enters a nursing care facility.

Reverse mortgages sound good under ideal circumstances, especially if the home owner has no heirs, but it takes an astute lawyer to guide the home owner/borrower through the maze of caveats.

# HOW TO TREASURE TIME:
# THE ONE IRREPLACEABLE COMMODITY

Making money before or after retirement involves using time efficiently. *After* retirement, if you plan to enter the world of entrepreneurship, time is even more important because you have less time ahead of you — and therefore less to waste.

*Time Management* is almost as important in post-retirement entrepreneurship as expertise and money. But there is one difference that you need to recognize right up front: There is little sense in being super-time-efficient if your body rebels at the strain. After all, when you have reached retirement age, chances are that you are not going to run the four-minute mile anymore or plan to put in 16-hour days.

Effective self-management at thirty or forty is quite different at sixty or seventy. In those later years the theory of time management may be the same, but the execution must be adjusted to the body's (not the mind's) ability to implement the theory.

Let us first look at two common ingredients of time management: efficiency and effectiveness:

- The efficient entrepreneur solves problems, performs duties, and cuts expenses.

- The effective entrepreneur creates alternatives, gets results, and maximizes profits.

An *after*-retirement enterprise will in most cases be a small operation. It is likely to be a home-based business that will place a steady array of temptations and time-wasters into the entrepreneur's path. *Time wasters?* Not necessarily so. If the wife asks for help in going shopping or setting up the table for tonight's dinner with visiting kids, if a senior golf tourney is scheduled for the afternoon, or if an old army buddy blows into town and wants to meet for a nosh and nostalgia — why not? But there goes time management, or what passes for time management under normal circumstances.

At age fifty or sixty or seventy you need to take the concept of time management somewhat more flexibly than you might have in earlier years. You can afford it; you should afford it for yourself.

But let us set up some accepted and possibly acceptable parameters for your time management. If you treat them just a little flexibly, adjusting to your own advanced biological clock, you can easily forgive yourself.

## TWENTY-FOUR WAYS TO USE YOUR TIME BETTER

1. Begin your day with an up-beat mood. Your attitude will determine how your day will go — successfully or drudgingly.

2. Don't sweat the traffic. If you drive to work, take it easy or, if possible, go against the traffic rush. Nothing is more gut-wrenching than traffic snarls and horsepower cowboys.

3. Be a creature of habit and start your day at about the same time each day. It tends to reduce confusion and uncertainty.

4. Get into the habit of making up an action plan for yourself, preferably the night before. Jot down on a 3x5 card or day book all the things you plan to do the following day. Number them in order of importance (subject to change the next day, of course).

5. Avoid early-morning time wasters. It is amazing how many people find zillions of things to do in the morning — from reading the comic or sports pages to discussing the news — before getting down to the work of the day.

6. First things first. Start doing the most important tasks first, while your mind is on them; when you are fresh. These include even those tasks that you hate doing but know will have to be done eventually. If you don't do them early, they will prey on your mind and keep you from doing other jobs — and they will have to be done anyway.

7. Complicated tasks should come first, just like less-than-pleasant tasks. Once the daytime interruptions start, it will be more difficult to do complicated jobs.

8. If you have the luxury of a secretary or assistant, meet first thing in the morning, coordinate activities, make assignments and appointments, set the day's goals.

9. As the Boy Scouts say, *Be Prepared*. If you've done your homework (figuratively, at least), the day's important tasks should go faster and in a more orderly fashion.

10. Be flexible, especially about deadlines (not appointments). Deadlines should always be a little flexible — especially at this time of life.

11. Stick to a reasonable schedule and don't take on any new obligations for the day. They'll throw you off your nicely planned and well-paced day and add pressure to your life.

12. Urgent interruptions are not always so urgent, except in the eyes of the beholder. Perhaps the interruption can be postponed or handled by someone else. Count to three before saying "yes" to unplanned activities.

13. Impulsive ideas can interrupt also. Try to bridle them, unless such an interruption can be refreshing or help to stimulate your productivity.

14. "Take five" can mean taking five or even ten minutes out for some other, unplanned task; maybe only to look at the paper or make a cup of tea. Older workers can achieve more when not bound to a steady diet of work and pressure. The pause that refreshes need not be liquid.

15. Block out the smaller objectives — like answering mail or making up a petty cash conciliation. Make a bunch of phone calls all at once. As in printing, ganging up activities can be more efficient and a real time-saver.

16. Complete one job at a time. If you do something halfway and then try to get back to it later, it will take extra time to get back on the thought track.

17. Plan extracurricular time as well. If you're out to lunch, plan the errands and stops you might have to make and do them sequentially.

18. Be watchful of busy-cycles. People tend to make calls, in person or on the phone, primarily between 10 AM and 12 noon and between 2 and 4 PM. Schedule your most important private work before 10 AM and after 4 PM.

19. At any age, but especially as a second careerist, you need to make an appointment with the most important person: YOU. Get yourself some private, quiet time occasionally. Close the door to your work space, whatever it is, hold all telephone calls, and relax, read, or concentrate on your favorite research. You need it. You deserve it.

20. Time experts say that you should check your schedule several times a day. One way of doing that is to set a small alarm clock or wrist alarm watch at odd times during the day — flagging you to re-assess your schedule, your work, your plans.

21. At day's end look over the left-overs. If you can complete one or several tasks, do so, instead of leaving it for the next day and possibly worrying about them.

22. While checking over the day's activities, see what results you have achieved. If you are satisfied, then all is OK. If not, what could you have done differently? What *can* you do differently tomorrow?

23. Now go on to plan for the next day. Set goals, priorities, and appointments.

24. It's time to go home — unless you already work at home — it is time to emerge from your aerie (or basement) to join others for supper or a drink.

## How to Prepare a Business Plan

The retiree going into a business of his own — either for the first time or for the umpteenth — will need a very detailed and realistic Business Plan. Even after decades of successful entrepreneurship, many business start-ups are run by the seat of the pants. Experience will often camouflage the need for such a plan because, frankly, it is a royal pain to prepare one.

If you are going into business to be successful — not just as a dilettante, not just to say to the guys at the club that you are a consultant or whatever — then you need to spend a few days drawing such a document. Here's why:

1. A Business Plan tends to get your thinking into orderly sequence. It will probably deflate some of your enthusiasm if your business scheme is unrealistic, or it will reinforce it if

your ideas and plans are indeed on target. It's like doing some serious market research before you spend your hard-earned money on a business that might or might not work. That alone should make the job worthwhile.

2. A Business Plan is a blueprint for your business. Like an architect, this instrument will show you how to proceed. A builder would not want to construct a house or an engineer a machine without a detailed blueprint. A traveler venturing into new territory would not do so without a good map. Look at the Business Plan as a map, a blueprint, or a light in a dark tunnel.

3. A Business Plan is an absolute necessity if you need to borrow money or even use the services of a business advisor. No banker or financial counselor will entertain a loan without a detailed plan showing that (a) you know what you are doing, (b) you know how to make money, and (c) your business can generate sufficient cash flow to pay back the loan.

4. Beyond the start-up period, a Business Plan will give the entrepreneur continuing directions. It can be adjusted to fit future developments and unforeseen economic changes. Like the Commandments, it is a guidepost to be followed for the life of a business, even if and when the business is passed on to other management.

When you consider that a Business Plan is both for the eyes of the entrepreneur and for an outsider who might be a lender, banker, or even prospective new owner, it should be structured to be quickly understood, clear, focused, and realistic. Obviously it takes expertise and thoroughness to produce such a plan. A professional counselor, CPA, or attorney can do it, but at considerable cost. $2,000 to $5,000 would be a fair price.

No matter who actually prepares the Business Plan or how much it costs, the entrepreneur owner must have major input in creating the plan. He or she must provide the bulk of the information — so why not try to sit down and plan it?

Here is an acceptable skeletal outline of a plan. It is a ten-step checklist that can be adjusted to suit your special needs.

## BUSINESS PLAN SUMMARY

Following your cover letter or transmittal letter, the executive reading your plan wants to know in a nutshell what your presentation is all about without having to dig through pages and pages of explanations and figures.

The summary describes briefly the key elements of the plan. It should excerpt the most important details and cover the following:

- Name of your business

- Business location and physical description

- Product or service, its market, possible competition

- Management (all members), experience or expertise

- Summary of financial projections

- If this is a loan application, how much you will need

- What such a loan will be used for

- Why this purpose is being undertaken

- What your long-range goals are

## THE COMPANY

Following a cover letter and "executive summary", we need to detail the actual business in two sections.

- A description of the business, its product(s) and service(s)

- A general but detailed history of the business, including:

  - When and where it was formed or founded

  - Legal structure (whether proprietorship, partnership or corporation — and if one of the two latter, who are the other principals or partners or founders)

  - Any changes that have taken place in ownership since the founding of the business, products or services handled, new products or innovations, acquisitions, etc.

  - Are there any subsidiaries; if so, who owns them and to what extent.

# THE PROJECT

This section is necessary only if you seek financial assistance. It will be easier to obtain financing if you focus on a specific project. If so, then you need to write about the following:

- Project description
- For what purpose is this project undertaken
- What is the estimated cost of the project
- How much of a loan will you need
- How should the loan be structured — line of credit, letter of credit, outright cash, et al.
- How will you use financial assistance that might be approved

# MANAGEMENT

While this section is not first in the order of presentation, it is first among knowledgeable perusers of this document. The person managing the business, or his management team, is the all-important ingredient that will make the enterprise succeed or fail. No amount of money can save or salvage a business if the management is not experienced and efficient. Here is what this section should include:

- Organization of the company if more than one person constitutes management
- Key management individuals, their responsibilities, personal skills and experience relating to these responsibilities, salaries and other compensation
- Other important employees and their compensation, benefits and, if important, track record with the organization
- Planned additions to management and the costs involved

# OWNERSHIP

This is the getting-to-know-you section, which should be quite easy to prepare. It will include:

- Your name, address, business affiliations, list of personal holdings and current values

- What is your involvement with the company
- What other owners, not involved in regular management, are of record
- If you have a board of directors or advisors, who are they, what is their area of expertise, what do they have to do with the management of the business
- If this is a corporation, how much stock is authorized and how much has actually been issued.

## MARKETING

When all is said and done, the best management and the most comfortable financing cannot move goods and services; cannot generate sales and ultimate cash flow unless these goods and services are sold and paid for by somebody. For all these reasons a section on thorough, sound, and credible marketing plans is vital — and difficult. In this section, you really need to show that you know your business. If you are new in your business, it will take some digging to come up with real answers — but when you do, you will have made a quantum leap ahead. These answers will be important to your business health. So let's tackle them, one by one:

- Describe your particular industry so that an outsider will know clearly what it is all about.

- What is the general industry outlook, nationally and/or locally — what does the future prospect look like?

- What are the principal markets that you want to reach — how big are they, what are social/economic/technological trends that might affect them, and what, if any, governmental regulations might impact them?

- Who are or will be your principal customers, where are they, and what will you be selling to them (or already sold to them)?

- If you have a track record of selling specific customers for the past one, three, five years, what have they bought and what has been the dollar volume?

- Do you have any contracts with any of these customers or clients, and what are the conditions?

- Are you able to accommodate these customers or are you planning steps to alter, adjust, or accelerate production and delivery?

- Who are your prospective customers, and how can you plan to solicit them; have any been contacted, and what was the reaction?

- Who are your competitors and how does your business rate in comparison to them?

- Your overall marketing strategy includes answers to the following: Pricing policy, credit policy, method of selling or distribution, service policy (if any).

- What is the geographic penetration of your product(s) or service(s) currently; are you planning to change this — when?

- What does your advertising and public relations effort look like, how much of your gross income are you allocating to these support functions, and are there are other promotional activities that you conduct regularly or are planning to conduct?

- Give a description of your direct selling efforts — including ways of prospecting, sales channels, terms, number of sales personnel, estimated sales currently and projected, cost of sales (where this can be determined) and market share.

## TECHNOLOGY

If yours is a specialized, technological product or service, a great deal of thought and patience has to go into this section. While you know all the ramifications of your technology, others who might need to read this plan will surely be less familiar with it. Try to "translate" your answers into basic English:

## THE BAKER'S DOZEN LOAN PROPOSAL

1.  Date:                  2 January 1994

2.  Borrower:              Your Company, Inc.

3.  Type of Loan:          Line of credit

4.  Amount:                $150,000

5.  Use of Proceeds:       Working capital for
                           first-year growth

6.  Terms:                 Two years

7.  Closing Date:          1 March 1994

8.  Requirement at         25% ($37,500)
    Closing:

9.  Collateral:            Equipment (25%), A/R
                           (75%) (see collateral analysis)

10. Proposed Rate:         Prime plus two percent
                           of outstanding balance,
                           payable monthly

11. Repayment             Interest only, monthly,
    Schedule:             commencing 1 May 1994;
                          repayment of principal,
                          commencing 1 March 1995
                          as possible, but no later
                          than 1 March 1997

12. Source of Money       Cash flow in excess of
    for Repayments:       cash requirements

13. Alternative           Additional loan covered
    Repayment             by A/R, equipment equity,
    Funds:                and inventory; private
                          and personal equity in
                          investment property

- Describe your product — is it in the idea stage? Development stage? Is there a prototype? What are the relevant steps still necessary to bring the product into production?

- If there is an applicable copyright or patent, describe its status, license, proprietary interest, et al.

- How will this copyright or patented product be affected by possible or potential technologies within the next few years?

- Are you paying royalties or other payments for the use of this product or process — and if so, how much and for what period of time?

- Are there plans for a second generation product that will pick up the profit momentum or meet changing needs?

- What regulatory or other approval steps impact this product?

- What are your plans for future research and development and how much of a budget have you planned for this R&D function?

## PRODUCTION AND OPERATING PLAN

This section is applicable primarily if yours is a manufactured item. This is, of course, a complicating factor which might not occur too frequently at this stage in your life. The greater likelihood is that your production will be either a very limited operation or subcontracted to an off-site facility. In either event, a statement is required so that the potential examining financial officer or consultant can properly gauge your operation:

- How will your company perform production and delivery of the products and/or services?

- Describe your physical facilities — size, location, lease.

- Will any capital improvements be needed; what will they be; what is their estimated cost?

- Who are your suppliers, what will you purchase from them, are any contracts in existence, is delivery assured, and is pricing firm and for what period of time?

- If labor is a factor, what is the local labor supply, what is its stability and availability, is there a union, and what are the contractual fringe benefits?

- What technological skills are required in the production of your products and are people available, or can they be trained, to meet your needs?

- What are the separate costs for labor, materials, manufacturing, and delivery costs — and how will these costs shape up for the near future?

- How do you see your production and delivery capabilities in relation to competitors?

- Can you note how costs will be affected by increasing or decreasing volume?

- Make a production graph for your *anticipated* next year or two.

## FINANCIAL PLAN AND PROJECTION

While management is the most important asset assessed by financial sources and advisors, the actual fiscal operation is often the nitty-gritty of this Business Plan. If your money source is your own bank account, or if you have family backing for your financial needs, then only your assurance is needed. But if you go outside your own and family resources, you need to corroborate your financial acumen. Two factors are always vital: (1) a plan to make the money that you will need (2) a plan to pay back the loan. While the actual *loan proposal* can be reduced to a single page (see example following this section), it will be useful to run through a lengthier procedure first. This procedure will strengthen your own knowledge and prepare you for any questions that might be asked verbally in the loan process:

- Your accountant/auditor — name, address, phone

- Your attorney — name, address, phone

- Your principal banker — name, contact, address, phone

- Controls — what system do you use to determine costs and budget?

- What are your current cash requirements and what are they likely to be for each of the next few years?

- How much money can you raise from existing equity?

- How much money do you need altogether?

- Do you plan to go public and, if so, at what point?

- What type of financing or funding will you require, over what period of time, and what do you plan to do with that money?

- If yours is a manufacturing business, what is your manufacturing and shipping plan?

- The following corroborating documents will be needed for your own knowledge and for the requirements of the financial officer or lending agency:

  – Financial statement for the past three years, if you have been in business that long

  – Financial statement for the current fiscal period

  – Cash flow projection for the current period, including the entire period of the proposed loan, preferably on a month-by-month basis (at least for the current year)

  – Balance sheet, income statement and statement of changes in financial position during past two years, and within the anticipated loan period

  – Budget for equipment and other capital acquisitions

For an abbreviated one-page Loan Proposal, see the following figure. This type of document is gaining in popularity, especially with companies or individual applicants who are well known or have a favorable track record. Because of its brevity, it invariably needs to be implemented by personal conversation with the financial officer or committee. It also elicits quicker response and helps to focus the applicant's thinking to needle-sharpness.

# STATEMENT OF MY NET WORTH

*Assets*

Checking account(s)............................... _____
Savings account(s)................................ _____
Certificates of Deposit........................... _____
Other investment accounts........................ _____
IRA account ...................................... _____
Keogh account ................................... _____
Pension or profit sharing ........................ _____
Life insurance, est. value........................ _____
Annuities ........................................ _____
Bonds ........................................... _____
Bonds ........................................... _____
Mutual funds .................................... _____
Stocks .......................................... _____
Other securities ................................. _____
Accounts receivable ............................. _____
Home equity..................................... _____
Other real estate equity.......................... _____
Automobile...................................... _____
Automobile...................................... _____
Jewelry ......................................... _____
Antiques........................................ _____
Art ............................................. _____
Collectibles ..................................... _____
Other items of value............................. _____

TOTAL ASSETS ................................$ _____

*Liabilities*

Home mortgage.................................. _____
Other mortgage(s)............................... _____
Money loans..................................... _____
Credit card balance(s) ........................... _____
Auto loan(s) .................................... _____
Installment account(s) ........................... _____
Back taxes (IRS) ................................ _____
Other taxes owed ............................... _____
Other taxes owed ............................... _____
Miscellaneous................................... _____

TOTAL LIABILITIES ...........................$ _____

TOTAL ASSETS ...............................$ _____
LESS LIABILITIES ...........................–$ _____

NET WORTH ..................................$ _____

# CASH FLOW PROJECTION

*Income*

Salary ............................................. _____
Interest or dividends............................. _____
Investments return ............................... _____
Social Security .................................. _____
Retirement plans ................................. _____
Other reimbursements.............................. _____
Miscellaneous..................................... _____

TOTAL INCOME ................................. $ _____

*Expenses*

Income taxes...................................... _____
Property taxes ................................... _____
Mortgage or rent.................................. _____
Utilities ........................................ _____
Utilities ........................................ _____
Utilities ........................................ _____
Insurance ........................................ _____
Maintenance....................................... _____
Loan repayments................................... _____
Transportation ................................... _____
Education......................................... _____
Household/food.................................... _____
Recreation ....................................... _____
Entertaining/gifts................................ _____
Clothing ......................................... _____
Savings account .................................. _____
Miscellaneous..................................... _____

TOTAL EXPENSES................................ $ _____

# L et us be

thankful for the fools.

But for them,

the rest of us

could not succeed.

—Mark Twain

# CHAPTER III

## FREE OR LOW-COST HELP
## AND NETWORKING

Early in the 1600s, the English poet John Donne said philosophically in his polemic, *Meditation,* "No man is an island..." Almost 400 years later, this truism still applies, perhaps even more so in this age of internationalism.

The entrepreneur, brimming with his own enthusiasm and ideas, will be hard-pressed to admit this, but admit it he must. Ideas are rarely the sole province of one individual. A true story surfaced recently about a Black businessman who hailed a cab in busy Washington, D.C. In the vehicle was a businessman who was headed in the same direction. The latter got to talking to his fellow passenger about his idea for a Jewish-oriented entertainment program on cable TV. The other man took due note of the idea and, in the weeks and months ahead, reworked it into the Black Entertainment Network. Eventually the company he formed went public and made him a multi-millionaire. Networking with another man produced this success story.

This writer, upon becoming director of SCORE's national marketing program, was invited by a local author to join an informal brain-storming session. The host mentioned his agent and suggested that I contact him with an idea for a business book. I did and it proved to be the start of a long and profitable relationship.

A retired executive who expressed interest in doing part-time consulting work, proceeded to answer numerous classified ads in the Sunday newspaper. After the tenth or twentieth letter, but one reply was received and that one negative. Evidently answering ads, especially for a retirement-age individual, was not the way to results. At a subsequent reception of the AARP, this executive was talking to another guest. The latter happened to be an officer of a consulting firm, and he was greatly impressed with the first man's background and conversation. He invited him to come to his office. Result: The retired executive received offers of field consulting that included a monetary advance, expense-paid trips about once a month, and satisfying remuneration for doing the kind of work he enjoyed doing — analyzing others' businesses and giving sage counsel. Networking again did it.

If a retired man or woman is thinking of becoming un-retired and going into a business of his or her own, then help is right around the corner.

There are both private and public (i.e., government-sponsored) organizations that offer specific help to start-up entrepreneurs. Among private counseling organizations are companies like Experience-on-Tap of Wayne, Pennsylvania. While this group is composed primarily of retired corporate executives who hire themselves out for short terms, usually to consult with companies in specific specialties for about $250 per day and up, they can be helpful in determining the course of a new business and answering sticky problems. The company was formed by seventy-year-old Philip A. Cerasoli, a former executive of several paper mills. More than 300 other executives, all over fifty years of age, make up the pool of available EOT consultants. This organization is planning to spread into other markets.

Similar counseling groups-for-hire may be found across the country. However, if an entrepreneur-to-be wants to have a sounding board about his upcoming project, or obtain specific advice on the direction his planned business might take, he can call the nearest SCORE office without charge or obligation.

SCORE is the Service Corps of Retired Executives. It is a volunteer association of more than 12,000 men and women, subsidized by the U.S. Small Business Administration. They maintain about 385 offices across the country and about an equal number of part-time, satellite offices. They will be found in federal buildings, chambers of commerce, and some colleges. With so many volunteers, most of whom have thirty or more years of experience, virtually any kind of expertise can be found. However, being a volunteer organization, the client-applicant must recognize that he or she must be very specific in spelling out the need for counseling and try to get a SCORE representative with pertinent experience. SCORE counseling is free and confidential. Offices are found in the blue section of metropolitan telephone books under the SBA entry of U.S. Government listings.

Many universities also have offices of the SBDC, the Small Business Development Councils. These are also affiliated with the SBA, but staffed by paid directors, often college professors, and graduate students. While usually lacking the long experience of SCORE counselors, SBDC advisors have available substantial federal resources in information, market research capabilities, and academic resources. Most of the services of the SBDC are also gratuitous.

The Small Business Administration, through its more than 100 offices around the U.S., has several other programs available to the retiree wanting to go into business. Frequently these programs are geared more to the existing, rather than the projected or start-up business. Other federal programs are supportive, rather than direct — that is, they will underwrite or guarantee a loan from a bank or an investment company.

The Small Business Innovation Research program that supports technical and scientific innovations with grants, mostly from $50,000 to $500,000, is one such division. In a typical year, 1990, more than 3,250 awards were tendered to companies.

The SBA's Office of Investment also supports and licenses nearly 400 SBICs — Small Business Investment Companies. These are private companies capitalized at about $500,000 to more than $10 million, located in most states, and owned by local banks or, in a few instances, by private individuals.

Virtually all states also have small business development offices that can render advice, counseling, site information, seminars, and frequently financial support. Most of these resources are listed in this book's *Appendix*.

Incubators are not just for little chicks; they are a great concept for new businesses about to be hatched. The business incubator is a fairly new concept, attached to and promoted by many universities to guide small business start-ups for a period of time — up to about three years — under the physical wing of the sponsoring academic institution. Small businesses may rent space in a university-owned building, joining several other "incubator" companies, draw on university consultant/professors and graduate students for counseling and specialized assistance, and share with other entrepreneurs in the same incubator building any number of activities — such as secretarial, accounting, computer, and research functions. Once the incubator business "grows up", that is, becomes profitable and self-sustaining, it is expected to move into regular commercial space and make room for another fledgling business. A National Business Incubator Association provides more direction (One President St., Athens, OH 45701; Dinah Atkins, director).

Many private or quasi-private organizations have offices, committees, and individuals who render support to start-up and on-going businesses. More than 4,500 chambers of commerce in small and large cities are very useful in entrepreneurial support and a membership in one of them should be weighed as a worthwhile business investment. Similar information and support can be obtained from the nearest Better Business Bureau. A number of national business organizations disseminate information and journals that are helpful, and trade or professional associations in specific fields are worth investigating. Libraries have directories that give details of national associations and directories.

One of the primary founts of information is the huge family of trade and professional journals, magazines, newspapers, and newsletters. There are literally thousands of them, listed by category and alphabetically, in directories available at the reference desk of all major libraries.

Some examples of media directories to use in your search for specific trade and professional information are:

*Standard Rate and Data Services* (Magazines, Trade Journals, Newspapers, Radio, TV, Direct Mail)

*Literary Market Place* (LMP)

*Magazine Industry Marketplace* (MMP)

*Reader's Index* (listing major articles in specific categories)

*Directories in Print* (Gale)

*Books in Print*

*Business Information Sourcebook* (John Wiley, 1991; Gustav Berle)

Small Business Resource Guide (Prentice-Hall, 1988; J.R. Mancuso)

Complete Information Bank for Small Entrepreneurs (Amacom, 1988; R. Christy/B.M. Jones)

Money Sources for Small Business (Puma Publishing, 1991; Wm. Alarid)

*The States and Small Business* (Superintendent of Documents, GPO, 045-000-00257-8, Washington DC 20402)

Seminars are also a valuable source of both learning and networking. Some seminars are very expensive, costing up to $500 for the pleasure, and possible profit, of listening to a national speaker for a day or even two. On the other hand, SCORE, SBDC, and chambers of commerce, as well as neighborhood libraries, often give small business seminars for free, or as little as $5.00 to as much as $25, if written materials and lunch are included.

Seminars offer opportunities for question-and-answer sessions. They are also great for networking with your peers, and many a valuable contact and symbiotic arrangement can be developed through such contacts.

Look on the bulletin boards of local libraries, large stationery stores, supermarkets, and pharmacies. Business and professional entrepreneurs often have opportunities to post their own business cards on such bulletin boards at no charge. Many civic organizations make it a point to allow members who attend to speak about themselves, exchange business cards, and give talks on their specialties.

One small business consultant who also does some volunteer counseling with SCORE as a means of widening his contacts, and acts as a "bird-dog" for a business financing organization, formed a breakfast club of area business and professional people. No less than 15 to 20 men and women, aged from twenty-five to sixty, meet once a week in a local hotel. They each report on their week's activities, exchange actual leads, especially about new businesses opening in the area, and carry each others' business cards.

Networking opportunities are indeed everywhere. They are limited only by the ingenuity of the participants, and their costs are minimal. Most of all, networking will make you feel that you are not alone — and for most entrepreneurs, no matter how self-sufficient they are, having human contacts is invigorating and necessary.

Remember old Donne's line: "No man is an island...."

## LOW-COST HELP FROM THE SBA

The U.S. Small Business Administration has available VHS videotapes that sell for $30 each — on marketing, sales promotion, and business plan preparation. In addition, there are 55 booklets, costing between 50¢ and $2.00 each, that can be ordered from the SBA Publications section, PO Box 30, Denver, CO 80201-0030, postage-free. If you are near an SBA field office, SCORE or SBDC office, many of these might also be available there. A complete list of currently available booklets follows:

### VIDEOTAPES

Each VHS videotape below comes complete with a workbook.

**Marketing: Winning Customers With A Workable Plan**
This program, developed by two of the country's leading small business marketing experts, offers a step-by-step approach on how to write the best possible marketing plan for your business. You'll also learn the best methods for determining customer needs, how to identify and develop a working profile for potential customers, and much more. PLUS ... the workbook that comes with each video provides easy-to-follow examples of how to use this information to meet your marketing goals.                    VT1    $30.00

**The Business Plan: Your Roadmap To Success**
This videotape teaches you the essentials of developing a

business plan that will help lead you to capital, growth, and profitability. It tells you what to include, what to omit, and how to get free help from qualified consultants. You'll also find out what an SBA executive, a venture capitalist, and a banker will be looking for when reviewing your business plan. The workbook that comes with each video includes a checklist of information to include as well as samples of the income statement, balance sheet, and cash flow forecast.

VT2    $30.00

### Promotion: Solving The Puzzle

Advertising, public relations, direct mail, and trade shows are the parts of the promotion puzzle. Each piece is important to the whole and each piece works to reinforce the others. This videotape and workbook package shows you how to put the pieces together to present a sound promotional plan aimed at targeting new customers, increasing sales, and getting the most for your promotional dollar. Learn how to choose the best advertising medium for your needs, write a press release that grabs attention, and much more.

VT3    $30.00

## PUBLICATIONS
## PRODUCTS/IDEAS/INVENTIONS

### Ideas Into Dollars

This publication identifies the main challenges in product development and provides a list of resources to help inventors and innovators take their ideas into the marketplace.

PI1    $2.00

### Avoiding Patent, Trademark And Copyright Problems

Learn how to avoid infringing the rights of others and the importance of protecting your own rights.    PI2    $1.00

### Trademarks And Business Goodwill

Learn what trademarks are and are not and how to get the most protection for your commercial name.    PI3    $1.00

# FINANCIAL MANAGEMENT

### ABC's Of Borrowing
This best seller tells you what lenders look for and what to expect when borrowing money for your small business.

FM1    $1.00

### Profit Costing And Pricing For Manufacturers
Uncover the latest techniques for pricing your products profitably.                                      FM2    $1.00

### Basic Budgets For Profit Planning
This publication takes the worry out of putting together a comprehensive budgeting system to monitor your profits and assess your financial operations.           FM3    $1.00

### Understanding Cash Flow
The owner/manager is shown how to plan for the movement of cash through the business and thus plan for future requirements.                                      FM4    $1.00

### A Venture Capital Primer For Small Business
Learn what venture capital resources are available and how to develop a proposal for obtaining these funds.

FM5    $0.50

### Accounting Services For Small Service Firms
Sample profit/loss statements are used to illustrate how accounting services can help expose and correct trouble spots in business financial records.                     FM6    $0.50

### Analyze Your Records To Reduce Costs
Understand the nature of expenses and how they interrelate with sales, inventories and profits. Achieve greater profits through more efficient use of the dollar.     FM7    $0.50

### Budgeting In A Small Service Firm
Learn how to set up and keep sound financial records. Study how to effectively use journals, ledgers and charts to increase profits.                                          FM8    $0.50

### Sound Cash Management And Borrowing
Avoid a "crash crisis" through proper use of cash budgets, cash flow projections and planned borrowing concepts.
FM9 $0.50

### Record Keeping In A Small Business
Need some basic advice on setting up a useful record keeping system? This publication describes how. FM10 $1.00

### Simple Break-Even Analysis For Small Stores
Learn how "break-even analysis" enables the manager/ owner to make better decisions concerning sales, profits and costs. FM11 $1.00

### A Pricing Checklist For Small Retailers
The owner/manager of a small retail business can use this checklist to apply proven pricing strategies that can lead to profits. FM12 $1.00

### Pricing Your Products And Services Profitably
Discusses how to price your products profitably, plus various pricing techniques and when to use them. FM13 $1.00

## MANAGEMENT AND PLANNING

### Effective Business Communications
Explains the importance of business communications and the valuable role they play in business. MP1 $0.50

### Locating Or Relocating Your Business
Learn how a company's market, available labor force, transportation and raw materials are affected when selecting a business location. MP2 $1.00

### Problems In Managing A Family-Owned Business
Specific problems exist when attempting to make a family-owned business successful. This publication offers suggestions on how to overcome these difficulties. MP3 $0.50

### Business Plan For Small Manufacturers
Designed to help an owner/manager of a small manufacturing firm, this publication covers all the basic information necessary to develop an effective business plan. MP4 $1.00

**Business Plan For Small Construction Firms**
This publication is designed to help an owner/manager of a small construction company pull together the resources to develop a business plan.                                    MP5    $1.00

**Planning And Goal Setting For Small Business**
Learn proven management techniques to help you plan for success.                                                              MP6    $0.50

**Should You Lease Or Buy Equipment?**
Describes various aspects of the lease/buy decision. It lists advantages and disadvantages of leasing and provides a format for comparing the costs of the two.      MP8    $0.50

**Business Plan For Retailers**
Business plans are essential road maps for success. Learn how to develop a business plan for a retail business.
                                                                                        MP9$1.00

**Choosing A Retail Location**
Learn about current retail site selection techniques such as demographic and traffic analysis. This publication addresses the hard questions the retailer must answer before choosing a store location.                                    MP10    $1.00

**Business Plan For Small Service Firms**
Outlines the key points to be included in the business plan of a small service firm.                                            MP11    $0.50

**Checklist For Going Into Business**
This is a must if you're thinking about starting a business. It highlights the important factors you should know in reaching a decision to start your own business.        MP12    $1.00

**How To Get Started With A Small Business Computer**
Helps you forecast your computer needs, evaluate the alternatives and select the right computer system for your business.
                                                                                        MP14    $0.50

**The Business Plan For Home-Based Business**
Provides a comprehensive approach to developing a business plan for a home-based business.                    MP15    $0.50

### How To Buy Or Sell A Business
Learn several techniques for determining the best price to buy or sell a small business.  MP16  $1.00

### Purchasing For Owners Of Small Plants
Presents an outline of an effective purchasing program. Also includes a bibliography for further research into industrial purchasing.  MP17  $0.50

### Buying For Retail Stores
Discusses the latest trends in retail buying. The bibliography references a wide variety of private and public sources of information.  MP18  $1.00

### Small Business Decision Making
Acquaint yourself with the wealth of information available on management approaches to identify, analyze and solve business problems.  MP19  $1.00

### Business Continuation Planning
This publication discusses the life insurance needs of a small business owner and how important business life insurance is when planning for the future of business.  MP20  $1.00

### Developing A Strategic Business Plan
This best seller helps you develop a strategic action plan for your small business.  MP21  $1.00

### Inventory Management
Discusses the purpose of inventory management, types of inventories, record keeping and forecasting inventory levels.  MP22  $0.50

### Techniques For Problem Solving
Instructs the small business person on the key techniques of problem identification and problem solving.  MP23  $1.00

### Techniques For Productivity Improvement
Learn to increase worker output through motivating "quality work life" concepts and tailoring benefits to meet the needs of your employees.  MP24  $1.00

### Selecting The Legal Structure For Your Business
Discusses the various legal structures that a small business can use in setting up operations. It identifies types of legal structures and the advantages and disadvantages of each.
MP25    $1.00

### Evaluating Franchise Opportunities
Evaluate franchise opportunities and select the business that's right for you.                                   MP26    $1.00

### Small Business Risk Management Guide
This guide can help you strengthen your insurance program by identifying, minimizing and eliminating business risks.
MP28    $1.00

### Quality Child Care Makes Good Business Sense
This comprehensive manual developed by child care professionals in both private and public sectors, explains the business and academic dimensions of operating a child care center.
MP29    $2.00

## MARKETING

### Creative Selling: The Competitive Edge
Explains how to use creative selling techniques to increase profits.                                          MT1    $0.50

### Marketing For Small Business: An Overview
Provides an overview of marketing concepts and contains an extensive bibliography of sources covering the subject of marketing.                                       MT2    $1.00

### Is The Independent Sales Agent For You?
Provides guidelines that help determine if a sales agent is needed. It also provides pointers on how to choose one.
MT3    $0.50

### Marketing Checklist For Small Retailers
A checklist of important questions covering the areas of customer analysis, buying, pricing, promotion and other factors in the retail marketing process.              MT4    $1.00

### Researching Your Market
Learn inexpensive techniques that you can apply to gather facts about your customer base and how to expand it.
MT8   $1.00

### Selling By Mail Order
Provides basic information on how to run a successful mail order business. Includes information on product selection, pricing, testing and writing effective advertisements.
MT9   $1.00

### Market Overseas With U.S. Government Help
Increase sales and profits overseas. Learn about the programs available to help small businesses break into the world of exporting.
MT10   1.00

### Advertising
Advertising is critical to the success of any small business. Learn how you can effectively advertise your products and services.
MT11   $1.00

## CRIME PREVENTION

### Curtailing Crime — Inside And Out
This publication includes measures to safeguard against employee dishonesty, shoplifting, bad check passing, burglary and robbery.
CP2   $2.00

### A Small Business Guide To Computer Security
Your computer related assets need protection. This publication helps you understand the nature of computer security risks and offers timely advice on how to control them.
CP3   $1.00

## PERSONNEL MANAGEMENT

### Checklist For Developing A Training Program
Describes a step-by-step process for setting up an effective employee training program.
PM1   $0.50

Employees: How To Find And Pay Them
A business is only as good as the people in it. Learn how to
find and hire the right employees.                PM2   $1.00

Managing Employee Benefits
Describes employee benefits as one part of the total compensation package and discusses the proper management of
benefits.                                        PM3   $1.00

## LOW-COST SEMINARS AND WORKSHOPS

While privately-conducted workshops and seminars can cost
from $95 to $495, associations and government-affiliated organizations offer sessions for $5 to $25. Sources are the Small Business Administration and its subsidized agencies, SCORE, and
SBDC. There are hundreds of offices and satellite locations
throughout the U.S., usually located in federal buildings, chambers of commerce, and colleges. The blue (government) section
of all major telephone books lists locations of the SBA, SCORE,
and SBDC under "Small Business Administration", or call toll
free 1-800-827-5722.

Libraries are frequently sponsors of no-cost or low-cost business seminars, sometimes conducted by SBA-affiliated volunteers,
as are local community colleges that offer business courses.
Check the bulletin boards of your local library or ask the reference librarian.

Many business organizations, such as chambers of commerce
or AWED, the American Woman's Economic Development Corporation, conduct both short-term, one-day, and multi-session
business seminars. The latter organization, for example, holds a
"Start Your Own Business" nine-session seminar that is very
comprehensive. It costs $240. Application may be obtained by
calling the toll free number 1-800-222-2933.

## INCUBATORS:
## THEY'RE NOT JUST FOR CHICKENS

Incubators, in business terms, are cooperative congregate business facilities, usually located on university campuses, that provide space and support services to small entrepreneurs.

There are about 460 such incubators across the nation, spread out over 41 states. The number is growing by about four to six new ones each month, says Dinah Atkins, director of the National Business Incubator Association, located on the University of Ohio campus in Athens, OH 45701.

Being affiliated with a university, and sharing physical spaces and support services — consulting, secretarial, legal, accounting, technical, transportation, testing, and even morale — incubators are a tremendous boost to a start-up enterprise. The nature of the incubator lends itself to small technical and service businesses, but not to retail operations.

Statistically, the success of the incubator type of enterprise is one of its most attractive features. Current figures, since 1984, indicate that 80% of incubator start-ups have survived. This is almost the reverse of other, non-incubator enterprises. Some incubator groups specialize in biotechnology; others are for women only; but all of them stand a better-than-even chance of survival and success.

One example is the Golden Circle Business Center, which is located on the campus of the Des Moines Area Community College in Ankeny, Iowa. The center does $6,000,000 in business among its 26 tenants and employs 80 people. One of the tenants, Dan Truckenmiller, who runs a business called Test, Inc., says that "I absolutely recommend beginning your business in an incubator. Here you are not starting a business alone. You can learn...from other people...who don't mind helping you out."

The Center has a director, Wayne Haines, who adds, "We've had 57 businesses start here since 1985. Fifty-one of those are still alive." While most of the incubator start-up entrepreneurs are below age fifty, numerous gray-tops in their sixties have chosen this route to become independent or to re-start businesses after earlier retirements.

## JOB FAIRS FOCUS ON SENIORS

One of the great innovations of the decade is the profusion of job fairs conducted from coast to coast. A Job Fair for Mature Workers was begun five years ago by a number of co-sponsors at the Silver Spring, Maryland, armory. Starting with 500 attendees, it grew to 700, 1000, and 1200. On October 31, 1991, nearly 1,500 men and women between fifty and seventy showed up.

Co-sponsors were the county chamber of commerce, the county high-technology council, and the county Office of Economic Development. Job Support for Seniors, a cooperative group developed and administered by the local Jewish Council for the Aging, provided overall umbrella support.

The "matchmaker" in charge, Sally Kera, advised, "Job fairs are excellent for leads...Fairs are not for lengthy interviews, but rather for gathering information about companies." She added that the competition is increasing..."When you speak with (prospective) employers, you must be able to sell yourself. This is not the time for modesty!"

Military personnel also can take advantage of job fairs, particularly specialized ones arranged for active and about-to-be-retired personnel. Once such military job fair was held recently at Fort Belvoir, Virginia, sponsored by the local USO. It was attended by representatives from fifty companies that span the entire gamut of retail, service, and business corporations — even federal government agencies.

Executive director Elaine B. Rogers of the USO-Metro stated that "The Job Fair is a unique timesaver for anyone job hunting in this area. With so many employers in one location, it expedites the job search process." Military personnel, active, retired, or reservists, as well as DoD/government personnel anywhere in the United States can contact the nearest USO office to see whether sponsored Job Fairs are scheduled in their area.

They are great networking opportunities, and the price is right — they are free.

From the company's vantage point, job fairs are economical channels to good personnel. The employment manager for a sizable contractor has been coming to the local event for the past four years and has hired at least one person each year. He has never found the myths about older workers needing more sick days or medical compensation to be true.

"Some of the people we hired through the job fair," he confirmed, "are more reliable than many younger workers and never miss a day." Another woman executive added that unlike workers, "mature employees are not interested in taking over the company. They are just happy to be using their skills."

The director of a job fair related that businesses can save money by hiring older workers for senior-level management positions on a part-time basis. With twenty or thirty years of technical or professional experience, older employees prove to be extremely valuable assets. "And by paying for only twenty to thirty actual, productive hours, the company pays for no wasted time — in fact, saves money, too, because these experienced people require less tool-up time."

## IF YOU WANT TO GO BACK TO WORK...

Re-entering the workforce after retirement happens more frequently than one would imagine. Once you have decided that this is the way to go, networking is the preferred path.

First step: Check out the local senior center, senior agency, YMCA/YWCA/JCC; check with the AARP chapter, neighborhood library bulletin board. Check all your friends, contacts, former associates.

Second step: Prepare yourself. Be sure of what it is you really want, how much time you wish to spend in a job, where it is most convenient to work, what benefits might be factored into a job. Be sure to have a neat, professional-looking resume available if that is asked for.

Example: Around the Washington, D.C. area, the following contacts will be helpful: Seniors in Training Employment (SITE) in Fairfax County, Virginia, is sponsored by the Fairfax County Area Agency on Aging; Job Support for Seniors offers career counseling for 55+ applicants in nearby Montgomery County, Maryland, including networking and resume writing; Senior Job Co-Op is a District agency and lists seniors in technical, professional, and clerical categories at no charge to applicants or employers; The Jewish Council for the Aging is one of the most comprehensive programs in the area, coordinating with and covering all of the above programs.

The American Association of Retired Persons has a Senior Community Service Employment Program in a number of cities. Some of these AARP programs hold Senior Job Fairs. One such event in Atlanta, Georgia, attracted fifty local companies and support organizations.

Travelers, Inc., one of the participants, established a job bank, which listed prospective employees and eventually found many of them employment. "We find retirees reliable and highly motivated," said a spokesperson.

## HEADHUNTERS AND OTHER HELPERS

Retirement is not always a voluntary move. Many a high-flying executive has been pushed out of the nest without a parachute, golden or otherwise. If that happens, and total retirement or entrepreneurship is not one of the desired options, a "head-hunter" might be a good person to know.

A headhunter is not a personnel cannibal. He or she is a personnel agency that specializes in a narrow field and seeks out executives in the $40,000-$50,000 *minimum* range. They are engaged by the companies who are looking for a specialized executive and are paid by them. Because they work for the employer, not the job-seeker, these headhunters are tough to crack. It is usually *they* who seek out the executive, not the other way around. But not necessarily so.

An executive who has left his company, voluntarily or otherwise, should immediately research the top search organization in his or her field and call them for an appointment or invitation to submit a resume. Here are some examples of headhunter firm specializations:

Parssons, Maitland, Florida — Aerospace industry

John Sibbald, Associates, Chicago, Illinois — Hospitality industry

Robert W. Dingman Co., Westlake Village, California — associations and non-profit organizations

Heidrick & Struggles, Inc., New York, New York — Banks and financial institutions

Beall & Co., Roswell, Georgia — Communications industry

Houze, Shourds & Montgomery, Inc., Long Beach, California — Computer software

Ward Howell International, Inc., Dallas, Texas — Energy field

More information is contained in a recent book by John Sibbald called "The Career Makers: America's Top Executive Recruiters" (Harper & Row).

Major executive recruiting firms can get more than 25,000 unsolicited applications a year. Most of them remain unanswered and unprocessed. To get a resume considered, it should be addressed to a specific individual who specializes in the field of the applicant, and should be presented in a professional and acceptable format.

While some recruiting agencies "repackage" an applicant's resume, often for a substantial fee of several hundred dollars, the following ingredients are necessary:

- A cover letter on good stationery that spells out quickly and clearly who the applicant is and what his or her assets are, what he/she is looking for and in what salary range.

- A neat, concise resume that lists professional and business background first, in chronological order, working from the present backward.

- A good, clear, professional photo can be helpful in establishing identity.

- The packaging of your application in a neat protective folder; typing that is professional and error-free.

- A follow-up call within the first month is desirable, perhaps even within the first few days, to inquire whether the application has been received and if anything else might be needed.

Another motivation in the placement of temporarily "retired" men and women, or those who have retired, changed their minds, and want to go back to work — at least part-time — is the "rent-an-exec" system.

*Forbes Magazine* was one of the first to report on this trend. It pointed out that executive vacancies are not always filled from within, because that would create a vacuum further down the chain of command. Instead, companies will contact an executive recruiter, such as Parssons in Maitland, Florida, to "order" such-and-such an executive for one week, or one month, within a stipulated compensation range.

Executive temps culled from the ranks of semi-retired men and women have certain advantages which have made this system quite popular in many industries. Reasons for using "rent-an-exec" agencies include:

- Immediate availability of experienced people

- Set rates that do not include any benefits

- No moral commitments beyond the contract

- Easy replacement if the initial candidate is not suitable

- An easy and neutral way of assessing the exec-temp's abilty for a possible permanent offer (25% of temporary executives get offers and then convert to permanent employees)

- Time to train younger executives, under the aegis of the temporary, but highly experienced executive

- Utilization of top outside talent that might otherwise not be affordable

- Seeing a company through a very hectic but temporary period of intense activity, without having to make the investment in a permanent executive.

Other agencies that specialize in temporary executive placement, some of which have at least 2,500 names on file at any time, include:

The Corporate Staff, San Mateo, California

Executive Corner, Menlo Park, California
   (a Robert Half subsidiary)

Executive-in-Residence, New York, New York

Executive Staff Corporation, Denver, Colorado

Interim Management Corporation, New York, New York

Klivans, Becker & Smith, Cleveland, Ohio

Management Assistance Group, W. Hartford, Connecticut

The Pickwick Group, Wellesley Hills, Massachusetts

Princeton Entrepreneurial Resources, Princeton, New Jersey

Rader, O'Neal, McGuiness & Co., Houston, Texas

Robert William James & Assoc., Boulder, Colorado

Savants, Inc., Roswell, Georgia

Men and women who have not been in the upper levels of management but who have been "retired" before their time, also have opportunities to go back to work in the same capacity, in other assignments, as temporaries, or to take interim jobs while they plan their entry into businesses of their own.

The national Kelly Services company has a division called "Encore" which, according to their information, "brings back some good performers" who are mature or even of Social Security age.

The program recruits mature workers and thus shares the advantages of temporary employment with seniors who still want to work. They will maintain a record of employment and earnings so that those who draw social security payments are not jeopardized. Kelly acts as the employer, which eliminates fee payments, deducting only applicable taxes from a pay check.

Approximately 50,000 mature temporaries are employed by the Encore system, conducted through more than 700 branches. The manager of the busy Cleveland office stated that "this fast-growing group (of mature employees) has a lifetime of experiences, knowledge, and skills to share with...area businesses.

In some of the more opulent metropolitan areas and counties, the local government supports volunteer search organizations that can be quite helpful. They are worth checking out. One example in the Washington, DC area is an agency called Volunteer Opportunities for Retired Professionals. While this office concentrates on volunteer assignments, these can also be used as springboards to paid assignments or leveraged to utilize new experiences and networking contacts needed to obtain paid employment or knowledge for business start-ups. Volunteer "jobs" are discussed in Chapter IX.

## REPACKAGING YOURSELF

Robert Half, an internationally known recruiter and author on employment and career topics, offers a number of "success secrets" for men and women who are squeezed out of a business, often through no fault of their own. He suggests:

- Update your resume regularly and do it while new and exciting things are happening to you.

- Do continuous networking and keep track of all people you meet on regular file cards. The majority might never be of any help when you strike out on your own, but a review of this suspect list might reveal a number of real prospects.

- Analyze your job loss honestly and make self-analysis a habit. Knowing what might have gone wrong and taking steps to guard against a repetition of such circumstances can help you avoid them in the future.

- Network by asking the other person for a few minutes of their time and for their advice. Few people will turn down such a request; everybody likes to give advice.

- Don't let reverses paralyze your action. It's like having a minor automobile accident. Experts say that you should get back behind the wheel as quickly as you can. Acting sooner is easier than later.

- Make every previous contact a present opportunity. Even former associates and employers, providing you left without incriminating circumstances, can provide a networking lead to another opportunity.

- Be sure to keep your spouse informed of your plans and activities. You need all the moral support at this time that you can get.

- Keep every interview, even those that do not appear to be promising. Don't anticipate negatives. One can never tell when one contact leads to another one.

- Be creative in your exploration of other work or other opportunities. They say that there are many ways to skin a cat. An engineer who worked in the aerospace industry was laid off and, unable to find another job right away, noted that his former co-workers had no ready place to have lunch or snacks. He started a mobile lunch service. It became so successful that he now has a fleet of them.

*C*hoose

*a business you love,*

*and you will*

*never have to work*

*a day in your life.*

—after Confucius

# CHAPTER IV

Most retirement careers are solitary efforts. A former corporate executive, the seller of a moderate-sized business, the pensioner of a career in the military or civil service — any one of these is likely to try his hand at becoming a consultant.

His or her retirement activities in the business world will probably not be full-time or as strenuous as in prior life. Still, starting a business of any kind is quite demanding. It invariably takes more time than anticipated. Moreover, the very nature of the entrepreneur, even the second time around, is such that time means very little and pressure is merely the lubricant to yet another round of achievement.

Considering the demands and pressure of a business — and even a retirement-age enterprise has demands that are almost inevitable — one's physical and mental health are very real concerns.

Experience and motivation are helpmates that will enable the gray-top entrepreneur to work smarter, not harder. Still, many hours of work go into the launching of a money-producing operation — and it is more likely to accelerate in its demands, rather than diminish. Consideration of one's physical health, mental attitudes, spousal approval, and relationship to children are all conditions to be factored into the ultimate decision.

In this decade, start-up entrepreneurs can range in age from forty to seventy. In the younger years, retirees from twenty years in the military, or thirty years in civil service, "retire" with good skills, robust health, a comfortable severance sum or pension,

81

and active ambitions to cut loose the restraints of their previous jobs and segue into a business of their own.

Corporate mergers, early retirement temptations, and enticing golden parachutes bring tens of thousands of managers and executives into the marketplace. Many, again, are well-financed with lump-sum payoffs, severance pay, or pension accumulations. They are also skilled and they are disenchanted with the uncertainties of corporate existence. The next step: start a business or buy a business.

Health considerations are usually minor with these adventurers in their forties and fifties — though family relationships will weigh more heavily in their decision-making than it will among those in their sixties, who also have social security payments to help bolster living expenses. On the other hand, the social security set is more concerned with health considerations, and less concerned with family necessities and pressures.

Starting a business after sixty demands other considerations. For one, it must be admitted that while the head continues to function well, and often seemingly better, the body says, "slow down a little." Hence businesses that demand a lot of traveling, excessive working on one's feet, physical exertion, or high tension activities and relationships, stringent deadlines, irregular hours, and interrelationships with "nervous types", might just have to be eliminated from consideration.

On the other hand, a business that can be operated from home, or one in which one's spouse can participate, can be beneficial to one's physical and mental health — not to mention spousal relations.

From an emotional and psychological perspective, that period beyond sixty can be clouded, or even pre-empted, with spousal plans that are in conflict with business plans. Maybe the other half has been looking forward to long-distance travels, vacations, making improvements in the house, or spending some time with the grandchildren in another town — and all these dreams simply do not dovetail with your own dreams for entrepreneurship. You will first have to settle those problems, perhaps adjust your business plans a little, and keep peace in the family. It is a sensitive time when many divorces take place and nothing can be more destructive, emotionally and financially, than a family split.

## "CHILDREN" AND YOUR
## RETIREMENT OPTIONS

Children are another consideration. Oh, no, not those little ones. At this age, they should be long out of the nest. But then you cannot tell. There are many well-documented cases of children in their thirties and forties coming home to roost, or to make claims, directly or indirectly, upon monies that you had planned to use for your own financing requirements.

Suppose your daughter and her husband split up; they have two small children and no place to go. You offer your home — there goes the space that you planned to use for your at-home business. Your son's business was totally mismanaged and goes belly up. Creditors are clamoring to take his house away — or yours which you put up as a co-signatory to his debts. His car, his credit card, and his emotional equilibrium are as much in jeopardy as are yours. It sounds like an unlikely scenario, but it has happened. What are you going to do? Chances are that you are going to pull out your checkbook or take out an equity loan and pay the bills.

Another scenario that is making its appearance in this age is our generation's penchant for a superior education for our children. This is a situation that might have occurred twenty or thirty years ago, but it is impacting your retirement life *now*. How?

The national columnist Jane Bryant Quinn called attention to this potential plight in one of her columns. She pointed out that baby boomers have rejected the traditional family cycles of having children in their twenties, sending children to state colleges or even community colleges, and socking away retirement money at early ages. Today, she pointed out, parents are just as likely to have children in their thirties, send kids to private universities and even private secondary schools, and "invest" their future retirement funds in the youngster's career.

Quinn decries this trend and warns against it. She proposes that today's "boomer" generation plan for retirement funding at the same time as college tuition. This holds true especially if children have been postponed into later years and now, at age fifty or sixty, it will be virtually impossible to assure sufficient retirement savings to make post-retirement plans feasible.

To preserve not only the prospective retirees' mental health and fiscal health, Mrs. Quinn suggests a plan advanced by Richard Anderson, vice chancellor of Washington University of St. Louis, Missouri:

1. Buy a house and keep it. Accumulate equity that you can tap for college tuition. Don't fall for the trap of buying bigger and bigger houses with less and less equity.

2. Rather than college savings, take care of yourself first by maximum funding of a tax-deferred retirement plan — like Keogh for the self-employed, 401(k) plan for a company, or 403(b) annuity for a teacher.

3. If you have extra money after fully funding your chosen retirement plan, put it into a college savings fund. Whatever shortfall there is by the time junior goes to college, he or she will have to make up by part-time work or by tapping into personal savings.

4. Don't borrow against your retirement fund to pay for high tuition costs. That is too risky at this stage in life. There are alternatives to explore — lower-cost state universities, two-year community colleges (especially if the student is not totally committed or is undecided about a career path), or opting for available scholarship or student-loan assistance.

"Whatever happens," writes Jane Bryant Quinn, "you cannot strip yourself of money at age fifty-five or sixty to finance an expensive school."

The five-figure total was just the money you had planned to use for the launching of your new retirement business. OK — back to square one.

Hopefully, none of these scenarios will happen in your life, but I thought I would mention them — because I know of cases just like them, and all thoughts of starting a business were pre-empted by financial strictures and emotional turmoil coming, quite unexpectedly, from outside sources. As the Boy Scouts say, "Be prepared."

Starting a business *after* you have retired normally has a lot of advantages. For one, beginning with age seventy, you can make as much money as you wish and not pay a penny back to

Uncle Sam, the purveyor of your monthly Social Security check.

Another benefit is that your taxes are a bit lower, and that makes it more fun to work and keep more for yourself, of course. Some businesses that require start-up costs might not make sufficient profits to make up for the seeding costs. But that's OK, too. One business I started took four years to begin making money, and that, I understand, is fairly typical of many businesses. If you start a business at age sixty-six, let's say, and you just manage to break even before you reach seventy, you won't have to worry about giving Social Security back one dollar of every three they have given you. Start making profits by age seventy, and you are in the clear. As we said above, at age seventy you keep everything you make plus all of your Social Security income.

During retirement years (this varies from person to person, of course), the entrepreneur is subject to the same insidious malaise as he would be during earlier years. This disease sneaks up on you and sometimes hits you with sudden ferocity — upon which you just throw in the sponge, often do totally irrational things, say, "the hell with everything", and just up and quit. This malaise is called "burn out" and it comes from "putting all your eggs into one basket." This psychological depression is something you do *not* need.

A lot of the pop psychology books tell you how to be successful, but only you know what your tolerance is. It is very difficult to examine yourself (no matter what your age), and even more difficult to bridle your ambition and pride, and admit to yourself that you might have bitten off more than you can comfortably digest.

There are some steps you can take to counter the malaise of burn-out. For instance, you don't need all that excitement and money anymore. You've already proven that you can be successful. So now convince yourself that the new business you are about to launch must include a half hour nap in the afternoon (if that is what you enjoy doing and need to restore the lifetime battery), and a week's vacation, let's say every three months. Those 168 hours, taken four times a year, do wonders to restore mind and body, and make your business something to look forward to.

Since burn-out is a form of stress, it can be controlled with a series of well-known counter-measures. These stress-busters should be every second careerist's ten commandments:

## TEN WAYS TO CONTROL
## ENTREPRENEURIAL STRESS

1. Set priorities — realistic goals that show you which must come first, and then do them.

2. Keep a time schedule for yourself — organize your day in accordance with the pre-set priorities.

3. Remember to use that ubiquitous two-letter word: NO. You might not like to use it when people make demands on your time that are either unreasonable or unprofitable, but it will be the only way to survive and do justice to your business and family.

4. Unavoidable stress will always be present and you will just have to roll with the punches — learn from each incident so that you won't need to repeat it. As the Romans said under such circumstance: *Illegitimus non carborundum.*

5. Identify those stress producers; make a list of them — and then go around them as far as is feasible.

6. Split these stress producers into two groups — divide and conquer — avoid those that you cannot control, and control those that you can influence.

7. Your time and talents can probably handle most of these stress producers, especially the latter ones that you can influence.

8. Save your energy (at this stage we must work smarter, not harder) and don't waste it on inconsequential, unimportant, and unprofitable matters. That's not what you are business for.

9. Remember an earlier chapter: No man is an island. If you need to know something, do something, achieve something — ask questions, get help, share problems with others.

10. And when all is said and done, re-read the previous part of this chapter — the part about taking a nap or planning periodic vacations. Enjoy your personal, non-business activities, too, because today is the first day of the rest of your life!

## BURN-OUT AND WEDDED BLISS

Marriage burn-out and career burn-out are like second cousins. They affect each other, because they are usually caused by the same circumstances — high expectations from yourself and others, nurtured by ideals that are crushed by the stressful reality of daily living and working.

At your job or in your business, you usually make your best effort. Chances are that you spend more prime hours at work than at home with your spouse. During the workday you spend time with customers, clients, and co-workers; you are polite, smile, think hard, exert energy, and are attentive.

Not so at home. Once you get home, you can kick off the shoes along with the polite facade. You can be yourself. You don't want to hear any more problems and troubles. Somehow, you feel, marriage will take care of itself. But it doesn't.

Burnout can spill over from work to marriage, as well as from marriage to work. If either of them is troublesome, the other is usually affected. If a marriage goes sour, you might escape into work — putting in long hours, looking for time away. When work becomes burdensome, you need to unload yourself at home and the marriage relationship suffers.

If either of them becomes faulty, a crisis on either end can become disastrous, because then you have nothing to fall back upon. Burnout must be anticipated, on either end. When it inundates you from both sides, something will give — you are either fired, you quit, you go bankrupt, or you get a divorce.

# CUSTOMER CREED

*The Customer is our reason for being here.*

*It takes months to find a Customer; seconds to lose one.*

*Always be courteous and polite during each Customer contact; honey always attracts more than vinegar.*

*Always do more than is expected when we handle a Customer's problem, for at this moment, it is his principal concern.*

*Never promise more than we can deliver; it is easier to surprise a Customer with our good will, than to disappoint him with our shortcomings.*

*Continually look for ways to improve quality and add value to products our Customers purchase.*

# CHAPTER V

## STRETCHING THE BUCKS

Going into business requires *some* money. One good aspect of becoming an entrepreneur late in life is that you have accumulated enough so that you can live off your own money — Social Security, pension proceeds, interest on savings, and dividends on investments; perhaps a paid-up domicile, a paid-for car, lesser insurance premiums, and, generally, lower need for acquisitions. If you need to borrow less money, you will have to pay back less money, and your interest payments will be lower, too.

There are other advantages. Presumably, in addition to all the advantages that come with the dubious advantage of aging, we have grown a little smarter and wiser. We are now better able to handle the money we have, buy more astutely, have fewer temptations, and certainly lower needs (other than health care).

In addition, the kind of business we are likely to start at this stage in life probably requires a great deal less capital than a more capital-intensive business we might have nurtured during earlier years. Most likely it will be a service business (such as becoming a consultant) or a business providing creative functions, producing products that we either invented, made in the garage or kitchen, or innovations that could be sold via modest mail order ads.

At retirement, we have available to us, in many cases, assets that can be collateralized. A paid-up home, perhaps a vacation

89

home, a paid-up car, paid-up insurance policies, investments that have accumulated greater value, and a more substantial credit rating — all factors that can be translated into security against which banks and other commercial lenders will advance you investment funds.

The very availability of collateral, of course, carries with it temptation and a germ of danger. To launch a retirement business you certainly do not want to jeopardize your security. Your age, no matter how brilliant you are or think you are, your strength, and your limited time, all combine to make any recouping of losses more difficult, if not impossible. This is not being pessimistic, just realistic.

---

Whatever money you need for a new business can probably be divided into three categories:

1. Money you can save by living more economically.

2. Money you can earn by investing astutely.

3. Money you can borrow against accumulated assets.

---

Let's take a look at some possibilities in categories I and II. The major expenses of living are shelter, automobile, food, entertainment/recreation, health, taxes.

*Shelter:* Chances are that the house is paid up already. Taxes, utilities, and maintenance remain. On an average, $250 a month will probably come close to taking care of this, though this sum can fluctuate wildly between $125 and $1,000. Selling the paid-up homestead can be a fiscal boon, but is fraught with emotional overtones that often outweigh practical considerations. In our present time, rental properties can be financially more advantageous than ownership. Taxes have risen steeply in some areas; maintenance is more difficult and more frequent with aging homes; the size of the house is more than an "empty-nest" couple needs; neighborhoods have changed, often for the worse; and worst of all, the annual appreciation in basic value, to which home owners have become accustomed in previous decades, has slowed to hardly the pace of inflation, if that. What is the alternative? Many older couples have sold the old homestead, taken the one-time tax allowance on their capital gains, and opted for a rental apartment in the newer suburbs.

Rentals free much equity capital in an older, paid-up house— money that can be used to finance a profit-producing second career. Rental fees, while considerably higher than before (which is why more rental apartments are now available), can be accounted for more accurately in most cases, than the uncertain expense of an older home. Most of all, a rental unit usually offers easier maintenance. If there is one major disadvantage to rentals, it is that apartment space that is most desirable is more frequently found among condominiums. Of course, the latter eliminates, for the most part, the major advantage of a rental unit: the freeing of capital that might be needed to bankroll a second business.

In the final analysis, the ultimate decision is an individual one — and that decision is not always a coldly calculated, pragmatic one.

*Automobile:* In our younger years, the new automobile in front of our home or office was a badge of pride. The annual October ritual of perusing — even pursuing — the published announcement of new cars was a holy ritual. However, two things happened. First, the cars that we used to buy for $3,000 to $5,000, are now $10,000 to $20,000 and often double that. Second, we are getting older, and so are the cars that we are willing to drive. During the past decade, I acquired a $10,000 sports car, replacing a very pedestrian and practical station wagon that had cost $6,500. The sports car gave way 28 months later to a $17,000 small luxury sedan. Now, six years later, the last car still is very much in use and vogue. It gets maintained each year, corresponding to its annual use of about 8,500 miles, and last October's new-car announcement received not much more than a cursory glance. Aging seems to bring about a lessening of new car fever, and that also adds to the native capital that is potentially available to a new enterprise.

*Food:* Aging does not lessen appetites too much, though it increases appreciation for finer foods (usually more expensive), less fatty and bulking foods. If one really wanted to shop-and-compare at the local supermarket, compare the usual service markets versus the warehouse markets, and even the smaller gourmet markets. A $5.00 to $20.00 a week saving can easily be achieved. The weekly food pages and Sunday coupon ads all hold promise for savings from 15¢ to 75¢ each. All told, the annual savings do not amount to much more than an estimated $300 to $1,000 a year, but if the prosaic "a penny saved is a penny earned" still holds any validity, these very discernible and immediate savings add to one's capitalization of a business. Besides, doesn't it make you feel good to get a bargain?

*Entertainment/Recreation:* Now we can save a real bundle, each and every week. It is doubtful, though, that we will curtail the indulgences that this activity gives us by very much. The trend towards eating out has risen steadily for the past couple of decades. Proliferation of restaurants, especially in the higher-priced gourmet category, is legion. Still, with a little discipline and, most of all, motivation, we can save $20 to $50 a week, or a total of $1,000 to $2,500 a year very easily.

We like tasty Greek food, for instance. Within our area, we have three choices. We have eaten in all three. Taking comparable dishes and tastes, we have paid from $8 to $20. The lowest price was at a self-serve food court in a shopping mall; the highest was at a neighborhood sit-down restaurant where food was served by a waitress. Today a bill arrived from the credit card company which contained a meal we had at an area seafood restaurant. The meal came to $29. Tonight we shall have the same thing at home — fresh salmon filet, two vegetables, bread and butter, salad, and tea. Our estimated cost is about $7.00. Between one week and the next, we were able to save $34 on two meals. If we were to extend this practice to comparable situations as a steady diet, we could save almost $1,700 a year. Yes, we have choices.

Early this year we took a cruise. It came to about $2,500. This winter we plan to stay in and get to know our area better, visit museums, parks, eat out, entertain friends, attend a theater. Total estimated extra budget: $250. The savings could be $2,250. The choice is ours.

*Health:* This is a tough one. Older citizens spend more on medications and health products, and even health plans and Medicare leave certain sums to be paid by the patient. Health insurance never goes down, only up. If all goes well, one could get along on a budget of about $2,000 to $3,000; maybe less, maybe more. Getting on a good health care plan early on is of course a tremendous benefit — such as being retired from a government, military, teachers, or corporate health care protection system. But if you don't have these, you cannot turn the calendar back. It is one of the facts of life that health care in the United States is both spotty and expensive. Maybe some European countries and Canada have more benevolent systems; perhaps we are heading in those directions. But for the time being, this is not a category on which we can count to save a lot of money for our enterprise.

*Taxes:* Major changes resulting from the Tax Reform Act of 1986 might have favorably affected your tax payments. If your assets are above $250,000 it would certainly be beneficial to consult a trusty financial planner. Figuring your *net* earnings on municipal or tax-free bonds versus higher-income stocks or mutual funds will be important, depending on your income tax bracket. When your income is on the brink of one tax bracket, you might want to defer any further income during December to prevent you from jumping into the higher bracket. Keep good records or rely on on-going advice from a tax expert at this crucial period. Use proceeds from your IRA account to best tax advantage, again projecting your tax bracket carefully or getting advice well before the end of the year. Remember that earnings prior to age seventy are affected by your social security income; after seventy you can earn as much as you wish without social security penalties. Living in certain low-tax or no-tax states will also have tax advantages. Florida, for instance, has no state tax, which could save several thousand dollars a year, depending on your income. State sales taxes can be a consideration, though ordinarily not a weighty one. Still, if you make $5,000 in taxable expenditures a year, let's say, a five percent sales tax state would cost you $250, while a state that levies eight percent would nick you for $400 — and when you make a major purchase, such as a car or major appliances, the difference could be several hundred dollars.

Tax savings on home offices are substantial — as long as you can substantiate everything and keep deductions reasonable. In 1991 a new form was used by the IRS — Form 8829 — to figure all deductions to be carried to Schedule C. It should actually make it just a little easier to avoid complications and errors that could lead to an audit. Since many, if not most, retirees who start a second career work out of their homes — both for convenience and for tax savings — keeping realistic and complete records will be even more vital than it might have been in an office. Separate space, clearly defined as working space, and a separate telephone, a detailed log for automotive travel, and receipts for all business transactions will be absolutely essential.

---

The IRS is watching for the following items especially:
- Home office deductions
- Inventory, especially in manufacturing and construction businesses
- Earned income credit
- Business meals and entertainment
- Depreciation calculations.

---

Two important points need to be remembered about taxes: Take advantage of every legal deduction available to you; use a competent tax counselor if you are not familiar with the ins and outs of the system. Be especially cognizant of medical deductions, charitable contributions, and home office expenses. And, be "investment efficient" by figuring any investment at net-net — the actual after-tax rate of return. Always compute the after-tax rate of return when comparing investments.

Buying investments advantageously is of course important, but knowing when to sell can be equally important. Two rules of thumb are used by astute investors: (1) Sell when a company's earnings for a twelve-month period go below the earnings for the previous twelve-month period; (2) sell when a stock's price falls by more than ten percent. Since many stocks are bought for emotional or speculative reasons — for instance, when a hot new product was introduced — stocks should no longer be held once that initial reason for buying no longer exists. Portfolios should not be nostalgia collections.

And what is ahead in investments? The cataclysmic changes in Eastern Europe, led by the USSR, presage incredible growth. The historic events of today's front page news can become growth opportunities for investors tomorrow. Japanese and European firms will probably react to events more quickly than American ones. Yet everywhere demands for goods and services will continue to be strong and even accelerate, and interest rates, due to demand for investment capital, will not slide downward too much.

Such rapid and revolutionary changes in the investment market will offer many temptations for higher returns. However, nobody has a hundred percent clear crystal ball. Every investment has an element of risk. Retirees looking to improve their income should always remind themselves that only "investment funds", that is, extra funds, should be invested in speculative ventures.

Retirees, for the most part, should look for relatively short-term investments. The years are not there to count on fifteen-year time frames. Because of short-term time frames, investment funds should therefore be more conservatively applied. This calls for focusing on diversified funds that should provide more stable rates of return. Shorter-term investors should also emphasize funds investing in larger companies.

As in any investment, you should try to understand what you are doing, even though you might rely on investment counselors and financial planners. The library has the tools with which to research investment information, but only *you* can know what your investment objective is, or your risk tolerance at any one time.

## FINANCIAL PLANNING

The American Express Company's IDS Financial Services division offers a ten-step plan for retirees:

1. Assess your current financial situation

2. Define your retirement lifestyle goals

3. Evaluate your current housing-related needs

4. Identify and estimate all potential income sources

5. Understand your pension plan, if you have one

6. Evaluate your insurance policies

7. Determine the best health insurance program for your retirement, if this is not yet in place

8. Determine if you are eligible for an IRA or other type of retirement plan

9. Identify gaps between income and expenses at different stages of retirement

10. Invest in knowledge — study, review, revise, ask questions.

Nothing comes easy. The *business* of retirement, *successful* retirement, that is, requires and deserves as much attention as running a normal business.

## RETIREMENT MYTHS

A popular retirement and investment counselor, Pete Dickinson, lists nine retirement myths that need to be known — under penalty of financial disaster if they are ignored:

1. Wealth-creation is possible during earlier years, even while enjoying a comfortable lifestyle.

2. Home equity is not a hard-and-fast nest egg, because home values recently have declined more than risen. (According to FDIC Chairman Seidman, "The government will still be trying to unload homes inherited from failed S&Ls when your grandchildren have children.")

3. When you retire you won't need as much money as you do now — but why plan for a diminished lifestyle? Why plan for failure?

4. Figuring on a retirement nest egg for only ten to fifteen years — a spurious bit of pessimism, in light of current medical research and technological breakthroughs.

5. Paying less taxes during retirement — a rose-colored premise that cannot be predicted, since taxes on all levels have a tendency to go up rather than down.

6. Social Security cannot bail us out in years to come, because, as this counselor claims, SS is a "bureaucratic dinosaur on the verge of extinction."

7. Medicare eliminates all health expense worries — another myth as Medicare covers only 71% of approved expenses now and may very well reduce payments even further, as medical costs rise well above average inflation.

8. Starting late to save for retirement is not possible — another myth according to Dickinson, who answers such concerns with a special "Late Starter's Guide."

9. Money is not everything in retirement — other factors are equally germane, such as opportunities for a second career, where you will choose to live, what you'll do in your spare time, etc.

While Dickinson's counsel sometimes borders on cynicism and caution, he covers a broad spectrum of retirement concerns. For those wanting to explore his philosophies, a call to 1-800-777-5005 will elicit more information.

# I*t is magnificent*

*to grow old, if only*

*one stays young.*

—Harry Emerson Fosdick

# CHAPTER VI

## SUCCESS

Success by association, just as guilt by association, is a fact of life, regrettably or not. Every culture has proverbs that underscore this. "If you lie down with dogs, you may get up with fleas..." "A man is known by the company he keeps..." "If you want to soar like an eagle, don't travel with turkeys..." "If you want to rise to the top, you have to get off your bottom..." "The man who always watches the clock will always be one of the hands..." The list is endless. At this stage in life, when we have successfully grown to retirement age, we should not need to be reminded. But nature rarely changes and it is often well to be reminded that, as Lord Chesterfield said a couple of centuries ago to his young understudy, reporting to him on his first day, "Before you take your coat off and go to work, come and walk down the street with me." That was his first lesson and one we can all well remember.

## CASE HISTORIES:
## THE SECOND TIME AROUND

In the following pages, we shall take a look at some popular businesses that attract retirees the second time around. All too often, however, men and women who have acquired an all-consuming hobby or avocation can successfully turn it into a paying, satisfying, and profitable business.

You have read about the housewife who became known among her family and friends as a terrific cookie baker, or marmalade maker, or patchwork quilt designer. Eventually, now being an empty-nester or a widow, she turned her avocation into a vocation. A few years down the road a large company made her an offer she could not refuse and she sold out for more dollars than she could have envisioned in her wildest dreams.

A man, over a lifetime, perfected his work on a bandsaw to such a degree that his wooden, handpainted Christmas ornaments became famous among friends all over the country. While this was originally a hobby getting him away from a demanding office routine in a fast-paced manufacturing company, he was now retired and was encouraged by friends to turn his hobby into an enjoyable and profitable wholesale and mail order business.

Magazines such as *INC.* and *Modern Maturity,* spotlight such entrepreneurs regularly. Of course, the conversion of avocation into vocation is not an easy, speedy, or inexpensive one. It involves an amount of risk-taking. Moreover, the pressure of producing a hobby product in large quantities, marketing it, keeping records, worrying about deadlines, inventory and taxes is a totally different ballgame. But then running a business, and making money, is never easy — though one would assume that producing something in which you have become an expert, and which you have always enjoyed making, is a lot better than starting from scratch at an age when visits with the children, or nine holes on the green, is always around to tempt you.

Turning an avocation into a vocation can be as simple as writing your memoirs. Walter Swan did it. This 74-year-old storyteller of little Bisbee, Arizona, decided to put a lifetime of his favorite yarns down on paper. He had a book printed and then leased a modest space right on Main Street where all the tourist traffic streamed by. Naturally he called the store Walter Swan's One Book Bookstore, and that's exactly what he sold there — his one and only book. He called the book *Me 'n Henry,* which was mostly about his older brother and their childhood years growing up around Bisbee — sort of a *Tom Sawyer* book. On an average, Swan sells forty of his books each day. Pretty soon it won't be the only book, however. He has almost completed four more and they are being self-published, paid for out of the estimated $200,000 he expects to gross from that first one.

## THIS "FURRIER" STAYED HOME

Joseph Moats of Independence, Missouri, is one of those old-time masters of his art — which happens to be making fur coats — who are hard to find when you need them. At age sixteen, when he and his family still lived in Germany, he was apprenticed to a master furrier, where he learned this specialized skill from the skin up.

Two generations later, he still has not quit, but is passing his art on to his granddaughter, who is becoming a furrier as well. Grandpa Moats still works, however. He does not make furs from the beginning, as he did nearly sixty years ago when the apprenticeship program took seven years, but limits himself to teaching his following — restoring, repairing, and modernizing existing fur coats.

Moats works right out of his home, where he has fixed up a basement studio, and where customers from far and wide around Independence come to see the master. It's a grand way to continue his lifetime tradition, make as much extra money as he wishes to make, teach his granddaughter, and keep up with the world — all at his own pace and without any great investment.

## LIFE BEGINS AT 88 — AND IT'S GREAT

Tyyni Kalervo, as you might gather, is from Finland, or Suomi, as they call it there. She and her husband have run a neighborhood bar in the city of New York ever since 1933.

Mr. Kalervo passed away a few years ago, but his wife just kept going, running the friendly neighborhood establishment by herself. In 1988 her current lease ran out and the owners of the building had other designs on the premises. The loss of her lease did not faze Mrs. K. — as her friends and customers call her — and at 86, she went ahead and signed a new lease on a new site, just a few blocks away for twelve years. Of course, by that time she would be 98, but *skol* anyway.

Mrs. K. moved the big mahogany bar to the new location, had the tavern sign hung up, as well as the photo of her late mate and her own photo with the president of Finland, and went back to work in short order.

The place is called, of course, Little Finland. It is the permanent home of Mrs. K. You can get a beer here till closing time or sip a shot of icy Finlandia. You can even shoot some pool, watch Mrs. K. tend bar, and marvel at how a woman on the edge of ninety decided that entrepreneurship is a way of life, regardless of chronological age.

"What would I do at home anyway?" asks Mrs. K.

## COLLECTIBLES TO CASH

Stamps, coins, rare books, china, commemorative plates, vintage autos, dolls, miniatures, beer cans, posters, labels, and cookie jars — the list is as varied as it is endless. They are all subjects of collectors. And each category most likely has its collectors' society and newsletter.

While all collectible items have some value, they are subject to scams and unscrupulous operators who foist off imitations, or at best the real stuff at highly inflated prices. Many retirees have taken their stamp collection and turned this avocation into a vocation — traveling with small philatelic shows to hotels all over the country or exchanging information and stamps with other collectors, either for items they wish to add to their own collection or which they wish to sell for cash.

Eugene Pollock of North Bergen, New Jersey, was at one time a stamp columnist for a daily Philadelphia newspaper. As a lifetime philatelist, he continues to use stamp collecting as a way to keep up with the growing world, enhance his formidable collection, make new friends, and perpetuate his enjoyment. He may even make a little money occasionally.

Andy Warhol, the renowned pop artist, was an avid collector of cookie jars. Some of them were rare and costly. When he died in 1988, the auction of his jar collection brought $247,000 into his estate. This auction, says Lucille Brombeck, curator of the Cookie Jar Museum in Springfield, Illinois, has skyrocketed prices. Look in your own attic. Your old collectibles might be the key to tomorrow's enterprise — and riches.

## TOYS ARE HIS

The toy business, like fashions, is one of those boom-or-bust enterprises. One reason is that fads in toys come and go; another is that it takes many months to conceive, construct, distribute, and market a toy. By that time, kids might be wooed away by some other fad.

Stanley Cohen was only fifty-one when he retired — for a while. Having guessed right more often than not, he had sold out his company and "retired" a millionaire. But as a dyed-in-the-wool entrepreneur, he could not stay idle for long. When he started a new toy company, he vowed to stick primarily to basics and allow himself no excesses. Nor did he want to grow large again and lose personal control over his company.

Sometimes enterprises assume a life of their own and the leader has to go along or fall off the wagon. From being virtually a one-man-show, Cohen graduated once more into a $40 million success by acquiring a license to manufacture and market a different kind of doll. It was called a Cabbage Patch Kid and the rest, as they say, is history.

Despite his success with what might be called a fad item, Stanley Cohen stuck pretty much to non-fad toys that resist the market swings traditional in the industry. About 25% of company sales were made abroad, usually at higher profits. A considerable proportion, but by no means a majority, of sales were generated by large catalog houses such as Sears and JCPenney. The company philosophy was to turn out good toys, strategically marketed and distributed, and to try and anticipate, based on long, hard experience, what trends might lie ahead.

"It boils down to risk and reward," says Cohen. "The bigger the risk, the bigger the reward...it's a numbers game. For every ten products you produce, you plan for four good ones and one or two great money-makers."

There are other qualities that Stanley Cohen possesses that contribute to his successes — both pre- and post-retirement. They include being a no-nonsense businessman and a tough negotiator, being very decisive and knowing what you want, keeping management as simple and lean as possible (that means retaining tight budget control at all times), and operating close to the vest until you know the product is off and running.

In October of 1991, Cohen sold out again — this time merging his second company into Tyco Toys, one of America's biggest toy manufacturers. Until 1994, he intends to stay on as head of his merged company, Playtime Toys, and then? It is anyone's guess.

Trade prognosticators have it that Cohen will probably retire once more — for a short while.

## A ROSE IS A ROSE IS A ROSE

Gertrude Stein, who penned the above timeless line, has nothing on the Rose of Omaha, Nebraska — Rose Gorelick Blumkin. As a ninety-sixth birthday present, she opened a business in her home town. It was in a warehouse she owned, and the date was December 1989. The fact that she was then ninety-six and in an electric wheel chair did not deter her one iota. She knew the furniture business from more than half a century of operating the Nebraska Furniture Mart.

In 1983, Mrs. Blumkin sold the popular and profitable Mart to local financier Warren Buffett and his company, Berkshire Hathaway, Inc., for a cool $60 million. All but 20% of it she gave to her children. By 1989, family differences caused her to pack up and move out — right across the way — to open an even lower-priced bargain mart.

"I don't need no more money," the young-thinking, near-centennarian stated. But she needed work. That was her life — not retirement. With her accent (she was a native of the Minsk area in Russia, arriving on these shores at age twenty-two in 1917) she repeats her philosophy:

"People are better off to work than being retired. Work doubles your life...you must never give up." And then she adds with a smile, "The nicest people in the world are the American middleclass." And almost as an afterthought, "Don't be a beggar. Most people are too lazy, but I have more pep than some of the thirty-year-olds that work for me."

Needless to say, Mrs. Rose Blumkin's astounding success must be more than hard work. She *knows* her business and the industry, and the people who are her customers in Nebraska, and the adjacent Great Plains area, know Rose. In her huge warehouse, she flits around in her electric chair talking to employees and customers. "If somebody else wants to make $5 on a yard of carpet," she says, "I'll sell it for a dollar profit."

Evidently thousands of customers know this, making Rose's name synonymous with great deals on furniture and carpeting. Her grandson Barry stated that "My grandmother needs to work. This is her retirement. Work sustains her; customers are her lifeblood. She loves being with people."

Mrs. Blumkin won't reveal how much money she makes in this "retirement" operation. Her bottom line is "making customers happy." This old-fashioned business philosophy evidently still works — at least in Omaha, Nebraska. Customers still walk up to her as she pirouettes around the big floor in her battery-run chair, get her advice on furniture, or merely say hello. If the customers cannot find what they want, Mrs. B. will as likely as not take the order and say, "I'll have it for you next month — and I'll give you a good price for waiting."

Even at 98, Rose Blumkin does not hide in her vast emporium. On many evenings she has her chauffeur take her around to competitors' parking lots to check traffic. Life must go on. On December 15, 1993, she'll be celebrating 100. Rose probably will welcome you if you care to drop in.

## TEMPS IN TUCSON ARE PERMANENT

Robert Rheinhart was fifty-eight when he retired from the life insurance and brokerage business in Dayton, Ohio, and moved to sunny Tucson, Arizona. Following the customary spell of chasing little white balls around the golf course and enjoying his early retirement, the work ethic caught up with him.

What became obvious to Rheinhart was the large number of men and women in Tucson that had retired, but were not totally happy. Many men and women were hankering to go back to work, perhaps not to the same grind as in younger years, but at least part of the time. Hundreds of skills were available here, and it was only a matter of finding slots in the area's growing industry and commerce in which such skills could be utilized.

In 1978, Retiree Skills, Inc., a temporary employment agency, was formed to match-make the over-fifty-year-olds with employment needs in local offices, tourist establishments, and industry. The business was evidently needed in Tucson, because it prospered steadily, being affected, as all other businesses, by such temporary recessions as we experienced in 1990-1992.

Many areas, such as Southern California, the Washington, DC market, and Florida, are home to large numbers of retirees who want to become active again, but do not choose to go into a business of their own. For them a temporary employment agency, usually called "temps", is indeed a helpmate. Rheinhart has started to franchise Retiree Skills and suggests that it takes about $15,000 to obtain a franchise and training. An equal sum would be needed for operating capital, advises Rheinhart. He can be contacted at 1475 W. Prince St., Tucson, AZ 86705; phone (602) 888-8310.

## COWS DON'T GIVE MILK...
## YOU'VE GOTTA TAKE IT FROM THEM TWICE A DAY!

That's the message Jack Wilner of Greensboro, NC tells his seminar audiences all over the country. "Effective sales results don't just happen — you've gotta do something to *make* them happen," says Wilner.

His well-attended seminars before audiences of other sales managers are the result of the typical corporate squeezeplay. His clients include Wrangler, a division of Blue Bell, which is in turn a division of VF Corporation, which bought out the former company and then proceeded to shrink the staff. Wilner was one of the victims, but he turned adversity into an advantage by starting a seminar business. One of his clients, ironically enough, is his former employer.

As a former corporate trainer, Wilner, a tall sixty-one-year-old alumnus of the U.S. Naval Academy, stated that "what usually gets shrunk the most is training. It's easier to hire an independent consultant like me once in a while than keep a full-time trainer on board all year."

Wilner's layoff was not totally unexpected. The trend in his industry was downward and he started laying a network of contacts before the axe fell. During his first year as an independent trainer-consultant he earned more than he did at Blue Bell. His fees range from $1500 a day to $8000 for a full two-day or more program. Those who object to his fees get to read a sign that is prominently displayed in his office. It says: "If you think training is expensive, try ignorance."

## AGE NO BAR TO PASSING THE BAR

Once Frank Solomon, a Towson, Maryland, retiree, had sold his retail business, it did not take him many months to realize that sixty-two was no age for retirement. He enrolled in the American University law school and completed its prescribed course in record time. The first time he stood for the accrediting examination, he passed the bar and became an attorney-at-law. That was more than seven years ago.

Today attorney Solomon is busier than ever. He never made it into the kind of large law firm that attracts his youthful compatriots. Instead, he decided to literally take the law into his own hands and set up a small one-man office.

Towson is the county seat for Baltimore County, on the fringe of the city of Baltimore. A few inquiries, a lifetime of living in the area, and the need for an honest attorney who focused on the needs of the poor, the elderly, and the hurt, soon had him busier than ever. Within a few years, he joined another local attorney to share office space and secretarial help.

The business of running a modest law practice that would also allow him the latitude of occasional trips and consideration for his sensitive health, made such an arrangement ideal for Solomon. It also gave him the choice of earning virtually as much or as little as he wanted. Becoming an attorney so late in life proved not only eminently satisfying and stimulating, but proved that age is no barrier as long as the mind remains acute. It is a beacon for other retirees who have maintained a lifelong dream and finally have come to see its fruition. In some cases, like Frank Solomon's, switching careers is possible — though it must be said that this retiree's determination and intellectual and financial equipment made the realization of his dream possible.

## WRITING MAY BE ON THE RIGHT PATH

This is a note by the author of this book, presented with as much modesty as possible. This volume is book number eleven, produced and published within the past four years.

No newcomer to writing, this author had been editor and publisher of several small magazines and newspapers. But never, in nearly half a century at the typewriter, has he had a book accepted and published. In 1988, all that changed.

Two years before the first book materialized, this writer sold his last publication and retired — he planned to spend an unlimited time reading, writing, and traveling. It was typical retiree-thinking and it did not work. Retiring for a person who has been used to spending most of his time at peak activity, often chasing deadlines, and working with one's mind, is an utterly foreign concept.

The next three steps came in quick succession, all within a year. This writer joined the local chapter of SCORE, the Service Corps of Retired Executives, and handled more than fifty "cases" in which he advised would-be entrepreneurs on how to go into business, or how to continue their preparation, if they proved to be unready for this big step into independence.

A few months later, he stopped in Washington, DC, on his way to Baltimore to visit with the SCORE headquarters office. The unannounced stop led to a lunch invitation with the national office's director. Within a couple of hours he had an invitation from the director to move from his home in Florida to Washington and become the large organization's communications director. Within a few months he did, settling in at this SBA-subsidized organization.

It was not long before calls came in from all over the country, seeking advice and posing problems to be solved. One of them was from a publisher on the West Coast requesting information that only a Washington insider could provide. It led to collaboration on a book that proved to be a durable and moderate best-seller, entitled *Free Help from Uncle Sam.*

The other call came from a local author who invited this writer to join a board of advisors. This contact in turn led to meeting a literary agent in New Jersey-New York and, within a few weeks, to the acceptance of a proposal for a business book. This book, *The Do-It-Yourself Businessbook,* was published the following year and was soon followed by a string of others via three major New York publishing houses.

*This* book is number eleven, and several other proposals for additional books are in the hopper to keep this writer busy for years to come. It has not proven a path to opulence and riches, but a marvelous means to satisfaction, moderate income, pride, and opportunity to meet some wonderful people. Beyond these evident advantages, it provided opportunity to complete long-delayed work for the award of a PhD and, most of all, a reason for getting up in the morning, any morning, and letting ideas flow from brain through fingers — and seeing satisfying results.

Writing has proven a great way to keep busy, to make extra money, and to keep one's ego up. Book-writing has led to writing occasional articles for magazines, opened up possibilities for teaching and seminars, and it is a business (yes, it *is* a business, if you take it seriously!) that an appropriately talented individual can conduct anywhere he or she wants to roost. Its up-front investment is low and its time demands are totally flexible.

Writing might just be the right retirement career for you — if you've got the write stuff.

## *E PLURIBUS UNUM:* STRENGTH IN NUMBERS

Janesville, Wisconsin is a town of about 50,000 souls, south of Madison, near the Illinois border. Making quality products is still a prerequisite here and the Wisconsin Wagon Company is known for building the best little coaster wagons in America.

One reason the company survives in this age of automation and impersonal relations is that it still sticks to the old-fashioned way of making its products by hand — and by the people who are employed there. These employees are all elderly, most of them retirees who have opted to go back to work. They work without pressure. They work an average of twenty hours a week on flexible schedules. Yet the work gets done and gets done beautifully.

Al and Lois Hough own the company. States Mr. Hough, "I've got the best workers possible. They don't have to work; they *want* to work; and they want to work well...Everyone seeks quality."

In the old brick warehouse where the company operates, half a dozen happy employees produce at their own pace, working together smoothly and agreeing that theirs is a "creative and satisfying job." They build yesterday's products with yesterday's methods, but they build them well and customers all over the country appreciate them.

"When you get done," says Al Hough, "you stand back and say, 'Boy, doesn't that look great?' We aren't too modest here... When you finish one, it is absolutely beautiful." Any boy who is lucky enough to own a WWC wagon can have his grandfather relate how these wagons were the fastest in town — back in the '20s and '30s.

## OPPORTUNITIES FOR SECOND CAREERISTS:
## BECOMING A CONSULTANT

One of the most logical steps for a retiree going into business again is to become a consultant in his field of expertise. After all, he is likely to have contacts, credibility, and knowledge in an activity at which he has worked for many years. Becoming a consultant is also the easiest "business" to get into. It requires relatively little investment, no special location, and can be conducted pretty much at the convenience of the consultant.

If there is any negative aspect to becoming a consultant, it is the consultant's built-in problem: un-directed activity, apathy, not having enough connections, and a tendency to say, "Oh well, if I don't make that call or write that letter, today, I can always do it tomorrow."

To become a consultant successfully, one should start networking even before retirement. If a prospective consultant plans to leave a company, connections and contacts should be established preferably before the final day of handshakes and good-byes. It is possible, and this has happened frequently, that a departing executive makes an agreement with his old company, as well as with customers, clients, and suppliers, to continue on as a paid-by-the-hour consultant. This is especially true in government service.

Pricing one's services is vital if the retiree wishes to make income from his consulting expertise. Unlike corporate service, an independent, individual consultant does not have an infrastructure to answer phone calls, write letters, do the filing, and take care of the innumerable, and often unaccounted for, little tasks that make a working day disappear so quickly. For this reason, a consultant must establish a cost factor for his or her services. As an example, if you wish to be compensated at the rate of $50,000 a year or $1,000 a week, and plan to put in an ordinary 40-hour-week, you need to earn $25 an hour. However, a cost-accounting of your time reveals that somehow you have only put in twenty chargeable hours a week. Another twenty hours somehow have disappeared — being absorbed by research, correspondence, billing, reading, travel, and meetings. So instead of $25 an hour, you need to bill out your consulting time at $50 an hour in order to achieve your fiscal goal. Realistic cost-accounting is the first rule of consultantship.

Consultants earn close to $20 billion annually and their use is increasing rather than decreasing — simply because most of them have proven cost-effective for specialized, short-term assignments. A consultant can not only bring expertise into another's company, tide another company over a certain seasonal or corporate emergency, speed up a corporate move, or inject needed efficiency, but can also become a psychological tool for greater effectiveness. While a company might have perfectly valid expertise in-house, bringing in an outside consultant who emphasizes and reinforces the company's policy and plans assumes an aura of authenticity.

Dealing with larger companies, consultants need to be a bit wary. Often they are called in because existing management is incompetent, has moved too fast, has made thoughtless plans, and is stuck for lack of answers or results. Carl Icahn, the notorious corporate raider and CEO of major corporations, states: "Corporate managers have built up tremendous bureaucracies, and in order to justify themselves, they sometimes bring in consultants to figure out what to do."

One of the best pieces of advice for consultants comes from the corporate vice president of a large food company, who was formerly a consultant: "Ignoring the troops can lead to disaster, especially if the consultant is ill prepared." What this means is that the consultants must talk with the line managers and note the latter's intuitive reactions. They are invariably right.

Consultants are rarely hands-on executives. For this reason a consultant is better off to advise, rather than getting into the front lines as an on-site implementer. It is up to the consultant to make that decision, based on his or her prior experience. A consultant should always remember that egg-on-the-face is a sure way to oblivion; egg should always go into the mouth.

Remember that it is the consultant's job to bring an outside perspective, a fresh approach, into another company's life. Consultants should not have the biases or limitations of someone who deals with internal problems on a day-to-day basis. The consultant is a sounding board who, for the most part, should lay out a plan for the client to accomplish something in-house, using the client's own resources, instead of paying for outside professional talents. If you can do that, you will have earned your fee, over and over again.

More than in any other retirement business, a consultant relies heavily on referrals. For this reason, it is crucial to completely satisfy each client, provide good value, and come up with some solutions to evident problems.

## ETHNIC MARKETING:
## THE "MELTING POT" IS MELTING

Since the founding of the United States of America, it has been said that our country is a "melting pot". Ethnic groups have of course been integrated into the business fabric of our nation, and partially so into the social fabric. Recent trends, however, are melting the "melting pot" principle.

The massive influx of Oriental and Hispanic people has created entire urban sections where native languages, signs, foods, restaurants, shops, and churches attest to the separateness of each new ethnic group. The insistence of continuing and even perpetuating the original languages of these recent immigrant groups has revolutionized our educational and political systems.

Never in the history of our country has such separateness been so pronounced. Previously, Germans, Italians, French, Russians and Poles, and of course English speaking immigrants from the British Isles somehow accepted and adapted to the American language and its culture. The blending or "melting" was always taken for granted. It was inconceivable to have an election ballot printed in English as well as Spanish; or to have a sign at a street corner, in front of a church, or in front of a public building in anything but English.

Today, even Afrocentricism is being promoted strongly in schools and politics, perhaps inspired by the ethnicity of more recent immigrant groups. Clearly these are trends to be observed and to which we must adjust. Business, too, must adjust to these trends, though it would be difficult for an "outsider" to penetrate into these ethnic, even xenophobic, circles.

But if your name is Kim, go for Korean business; if Gonzales, explore a Hispanic one. If you are planning a national or mail order business where you, a plain American, are more invisible, then you better learn something about ethnic marketing before you say "Buenos Dias, Amigo."

The Oriental immigrant market is probably the most parochial; yet it is fragmented into Chinese (north, south, Hong Kong, and Taiwan), Vietnamese, other Southeast Asian, Korean, and Japanese. In addition, there is a huge influx of East Indians and Pakistani — each from a vast variety of cultural, social, and linguistic backgrounds. Each group in turn has its own shops, language, writing, and cultural affinities. It would be virtually impossible to try to market to each group on its own terms, without being an ethnic member of that group — until, that is, that particular immigrant decides to adapt to American marketing blandishments. How many are there? The numbers are in flux and swelling daily. Anywhere from six to eight million is probably a conservative figure — certainly a massive market, if it were possible to penetrate it.

The Hispanic population, even though coming from no less than 18 different Spanish- and Portuguese-speaking countries, is more easily defined and targeted. Well over twenty million Hispanics now live in the U.S.A., plus possibly a couple of million more who have not been registered. In the decade of the Eighties, the Hispanic population in the U.S. has increased at least 35%, with no sign of diminishing. Since this group is so concentrated in California, Texas, Florida, and New York, as well as in the District of Columbia, New Mexico, and Arizona, it is possible to estimate the Hispanics' purchasing power at approaching $200 billion.

Hispanics adapt to their new country readily, but selectively. They rarely lose their culture and lifestyle, the way they socialize and interact. Conventional marketing to this segment is going to be ineffective. Doing business with ethnic minorities, Hispanics in particular, requires targeted empathy, sensitivity to their culture, more group orientation, and understanding of their tastes. Remember that Hispanics have their desire to be part of the American dream, a proportionately higher percentage of disposable income — and they have 3.6 people in the average household. The average American household has two.

If you do venture into the lucrative ethnic market, either *be* an ethnic yourself or go into partnership with one or hire experts who can speak the language — literally and figuratively.

## INTERNATIONAL TRADE

The exporting and importing of goods and services is a major facet of American business. It is true that a different skill is required for this aspect of commerce; that the U.S. government encourages exports with all sorts of assistance programs; that virtually every state in the Union has programs to promote its own products abroad; and that companies that have been in the export trade for some time report a higher profit ratio from the overseas transactions than from domestic sales. With all this, it is still a difficult and tricky business to get into — unless the retiree has been in IT in his more active life. While exporting especially has all the earmarks of excitement and profit, it is not clear whether this is a business to get into, as a second careerist, without considerable study, expertise, *and time.* The latter is the one draw-back, a luxury that might not be affordable to the about-to-be-unretiree. However, let's look at what some success-ful exporters have to say about this business. They advise the following rules of thumb:

- Export only top-quality products that require no or very little maintenance, are unlikely be returned, and tend to bring the overseas customer back for more.

- Plan your export strategy for the long haul. It takes time to de-velop confidence, connections, and sales abroad. It takes time to learn a new way of dealing with people of different cultures.

- Acquaint yourself with all the facets of federal and state government assistance that is available in the home state, in Washington, and even in U.S. offices abroad.

- Take plenty of time to search out a knowledgeable, honest, and active distributor overseas. Rely heavily on personal recommendations. Use local U.S. contacts as guides. Make sure of any legal commitments — they could be nooses.

- Use networking with other, more experienced exporters. Attend private, group, and government-sponsored overseas trade fairs, as often as your time and budget allows.

- Do your research thoroughly to make sure your product or service is indeed needed overseas, not available locally, and priced to be affordable in foreign markets. American products tend to be higher-priced.

- Have someone competent check out foreign laws and customs — before you make any commitments and shipments.

- If you dispense any promotional or instructional material, make sure it is professionally translated, is designed to be acceptable and inoffensive abroad, and does not reflect American ignorance of foreign customs and mores.

- Because of time and distance factors in dealing overseas, it is necessary to have proper equipment to transmit messages, replies, and orders quickly and efficiently.

- To expedite overseas trade and increase your efficiency, look into hiring an export trading company. Many specialize in specific lines and can open markets for you and sell more effectively and quickly than you might be able to do on your own. Besides, they might be able to utilize cooperative shipping and overseas storage, particularly with less-than-container quantities.

## MAIL ORDER:
## THE CHECK IS IN THE MAIL. HOORAY.

It sounds wonderful. You locate an unusual item, or even make it yourself, advertise it in a magazine, and await the avalanche of dollar bills and checks. To read some of the come-on ads in some publications, the mail order business is the ideal antidote to retirement entrepreneurship.

Usually it doesn't work that way, though some astounding success stories of mail order millionaires persist from the immediate post-war years when product shortages and surplus cash combined to make selling any novelty item a surefire path to profits. The Chinese have an old proverb that says something like this: To move a mountain, one must remove a pebble, one at a time. It's a little like the mail order business. It takes time, patience, hard work, money, failures, and successes.

Let's start with a popular example, the L.L. Bean Co. This is a two-generation success story — a company that sells top-quality goods on a 100% return guarantee. Even with its quality approach, venerable history of customer satisfaction, and tremendous volume, Bean's return-of-goods ratio is 14%, which costs the company $18,000,000 a year in shipping and handling costs. To remain profitable, this expense must be factored into the profit on its merchandise — along with the merchandise itself, operating overhead, advertising cost, and the normal profit margin.

Two major cost factors, cost of the item and expense of marketing it, must first be considered. Both must be researched, priced favorably, and made cost-effective. The mark-up must include all of the above items and then be compared against any possible competition, including local retail or wholesale offerings. If the numbers still come out favorably, then you have something suitable for mail order merchandising.

The great unknown factor is the number of orders you can expect from a direct mail campaign or an ad in a magazine, newspaper, or on a radio or television program. Averages cited are two percent from a general mail order buyers' list, to five percent from a highly selective list. Consider that when you send out 1,000 letters through the U.S. Post Office's pre-sort system, your own cost is probably between thirty and fifty cents per name, depending on how elaborate your mailing piece is designed. One thousand pieces will cost an average of $400. A magazine with a good mail order section and a circulation of one million copies would cost about $3,000 for a five-inch ad in their special mail order part. For $3,000 you can only afford to mail 7,500 letters. Which way is better? There is no sure-fire answer. You will have to test both. That's where experience, networking, research, and lots of money come in.

If you get two percent return on 7,500 letters, you will have 150 orders. Each order then costs you $20 in advertising cost. Obviously, selling a $19.95 item that costs you $8 nets you only $1,800. You need either additional items to sell in the same mail order package (like the catalog companies do), or follow-up with other mail order merchandise on which you have lower marketing costs — since you already are dealing with a customer.

A magazine with a one million circulation that delivers only 150 orders, gives you a return of 15/100th of one percent. Of course, a two percent return on a million would be 20,000 orders and would make you rich, returning nearly $400,000 at a gross profit of $240,000. These are the mail order hopes and dreams. Unfortunately, the realities today are somewhat different.

One way to test a product or service by mail is to look for publications that have already-established mail order classified columns. Advertising with carefully prepared ads of four to five lines, and timing them astutely so that they do not fall on holidays or rent days, can be one way to test a product, a medium, a price or your copy — vital factors that can affect results. Keep careful records of results and make your adjustments.

One more caveat: Do not, repeat, DO NOT, load up on merchandise that might or might not sell, or that you have bought too expensively to allow you a mark-up of at least two to four times cost. Of course, if you produce the product yourself, you've got the best control of all.

And don't forget that repeat customers are the best customers of all and the lifeblood of a successful mail order business.

## ALTERNATIVE LIVING: PROVIDING ELDERLY SHELTER

Riding the old-age (not the New Age) wave is Standish Care Co. of Boston, Massachusetts. Its CEO is Michael Doyle, who in just two years has shown the way retirement living facilities should develop in the future, as more and more elderly join the ranks of America's citizenry.

Only a couple of years old, Standish Care has shown that it can provide the kind of living space needed by many elderly at a cost 40% below that of nursing homes. Standish communities furnish facilities that include on-site health care, meals, and local transportation. It is an alternative to middle-income retirees who do not need hospitalization, but do require some assisted care on a daily basis.

At the present time two operating communities exist and several others are in the planning stage. Doyle's plan is to expand via joint ventures with hospitals. His first two ventures were financed by a $16 million bond issue.

Retirement-age entrepreneurs with experience in the building business and hospitality industry will find considerable inspiration in the Boston-based Standish Care operation — and a role model for a very necessary and potentially profitable enterprise.

## WOMEN ENTREPRENEURS

Motivation to become a businesswoman can come from many factors. One of the primary ones is discrimination.

The kind of discrimination we refer to is economic, not sexual harassment. Fact: The earning gap between the sexes narrowed during the 1980s, according to the *AARP Bulletin,* but income equality for the 6.2 million women over fifty who work full time remains an elusive goal.

The three examples offered in the AARP story involve a 68-year-old property manager who was unable to find another job in her field and had to take a $5-an-hour job in a bar. Another woman, 64, was a college professor whose salary was 65% that of her male colleagues with comparable tenure. The third woman was a 57-year-old former homemaker who tried to return to work after raising a family and being out of the job market for a dozen years. All she could earn was a salary one-half as much as those male workers in her field who had stayed with the company.

On national average women receive only 72¢ on every dollar earned by men in a comparable capacity. The reasons companies give for the disparity are (1) women over fifty are less highly educated than men in that field; (2) because women usually take time out for child-bearing, they have less tenure than men; (3) women have in the past usually chosen occupations that are lower-paying to start with. (Example: Bank tellers used to be primarily men; then, starting with World War II, women took over. Today, 95% of all tellers over the age of fifty are women and their salaries are well under those of men, averaging $304 per week.)

In the teaching profession, the wage disparity has closed considerably. In elementary schools women teachers make 94% of men's salaries, and 90% in secondary schools. Other occupations are becoming "infiltrated" with women workers who are learning and taking non-traditional jobs. This trend, however, is less likely to manifest itself among older women.

As young executive women age, they will become more entrepreneurially minded. Better education, fewer children, and a growing sense of risk-taking are generating a mature cadre of women who are increasingly entering the business world on their own. The business journals are full of stories about women who are hanging out their shingles and making good money. In fact, the statistics of survival in small businesses are considerably better among women than they are among men. The 1990s are wide open for women entrepreneurs. There is no speed limit for female entrepreneurs who know how to express themselves — with knowledge and experience.

## EXPERIENCE BECOMES A FIVE-LETTER WORD

M-o-n-e-y.

Harvey Gittler of Oberlin, Ohio, used to be a high-powered sales executive with a New York-based industrial company. When he retired, he chose a lovely little college town with 8,500 people, dominated by liberal Oberlin College. It is a scant hour from Cleveland and the big airport.

For the past several years, Gittler has been writing dozens of articles about business management; thousands of words that return both pleasure and dollars. His articles have appeared in the Wall Street Journal as well as a number of engineering magazines, a field in which he was well known. On occasion he gives talks on his specialty.

His companions now are the *Magazine Industry Marketplace,* the *Standard Rate and Data Service,* and a trusty typewriter. The telephone keeps him connected to the former world in which he was active. When he needs office services, he gets on his bicycle and pedals a short distance to the local copy shop.

This entrepreneurial retiree created a new enterprise for himself, as well as a comfortable and more relaxing lifestyle — with virtually no capital outlay and only as much pressure as he wants to apply to himself. Many a retiree, casting about for a second career and perhaps a little additional income, has Harvey Gittler's experience and talent. Writing and speaking are twin assets that make for very compatible inventory.

## GOING TO WORK — AGAIN

Not every retiree who is going back to work becomes an entrepreneur. Not everyone wants to take the risk, has lofty horizons, or craves self-determination. Many say, let somebody else worry about planning and marketing and making a million. According to a *Modern Maturity* magazine survey conducted in 1988, 35,000 readers gave their opinions on their preferences for a working life the second time around.

As writer Caroline Bird and her research assistant Marjorie Godfrey said in a follow-up report "...more (people past 62) than is generally realized believe in work as a way of life. Money is less important to those past the usual retirement age; only 32% of these older workers said they are working primarily for the money compared with 46% (who worked because they wanted to, regardless of the income)."

The report pointed out a 69-year-old former mechanic who went to work at a McDonald's as a general utility man, at $4.75 an hour. A 61-year-old widow took courses at a local hospital and became a practical nurse, taking care of elderly patients in her own home. A 73-year-old retiree, also a former machinist, is making miniature medical instrument prototypes with the help of a jeweler's loupe. A pharmacist, at 74, went back to update his professional skill and now works part-time in a local drugstore.

The report goes on to point out others who have completely left their original fields. A divorced homemaker became a $60-a-day poker dealer in a Las Vegas casino. A retired Navy officer, who served in Vietnam, went to divinity school and became a Methodist minister. A corporate manager, squeezed out with a golden handshake, became a hearing commissioner for labor grievances in a related government agency.

Health, oddly enough, was a cause for retirement in only four percent of all reported cases. Of those going back to work at retirement age, 53% do so full-time; 40% less than full time; and seven percent work just part of the year.

Getting the job at an advanced age is sometimes difficult, if not frustratingly impossible. Of the 35,000 test group that reported to *Modern Maturity* magazine, only 18% decided to go the entrepreneurial route — that is, about 6,300 new businesses were started by this group.

The largest group of respondents obtained employment through networking. Friends or family members recommended them in 26% of the cases. A rather surprising 17% obtained employment through newspaper ads, while 12% took the initiative and applied on their own. Only five percent went through employment or executive search agencies, and eight percent went back to work for former employers.

As for compensation of recycled workers, those who formerly earned less than $20,000 a year, went back to work at higher incomes — a sign of inflationary times, recognition of experience, or increased self-confidence. When you look at former employees in the $20,000 to $50,000-and-up range, all of them took lesser-paying jobs — in some cases as low as one-fourth of their former executive remuneration.

Of those retirees who went back to work in businesses of their own, most of them developed small service businesses that required small capital outlay, invested in low-cost franchises, or purchased moderate businesses. Among these in this control group were a woman who became a relocation expert, a man who went into car detailing, and another who created a college advisory service for high school students. A retired secretary, whose hobby was making exotic jams, went into the business earnestly and is now earning a comfortable $30,000 in an average year, selling to stores, home sales groups, and mail order customers.

Returning-to-work retirees are usually highly motivated men and women. They form a great resource for America, because they are willing to work and willing to learn what they don't know. For employers it is a valued symbiosis.

## FROM CLASSROOM TO COMMERCE

A university teaching and/or research position is an ideal jumping-off platform for entrepreneurship. Especially if the university runs a business incubator facility on campus. Many academic institutions are located in quiet little towns and that can make a business start-up the ideal combination.

Dr. James Gilfert has spent many years teaching and doing engineering research at Ohio University of Athens. In this lovely little town of 50,000, close to a state park and Dow Lake, 75 miles from the Columbus airport, it was an ideal place to remain and start a business.

The local incubator which "hatched" new businesses such as Dr. Gilfert's Automation Test Equipment company, proved a

low-cost way to get started. After four years in this location, the
new engineering facility and laboratory has produced around
200 traffic light control systems. They have sold to departments
of transportation in cities, counties, and states from coast to
coast. At an average of $6,000 each, it is easy to figure that the
new business has brought in around $1,200,000 gross income —
all the while the proprietor maintains his association with the
university by part-time teaching.

Most of the other incubator enterprises have been started by
still-active or retired academicians. The university furnishes low-
cost space and the opportunity to network with the academic
staff. The new entrepreneur, especially if he or she has been associated with the university, can remain *in situ* and get a real jump-
start for the fledgling enterprise. Again, an ideal symbiosis!

## GETTING OUT THE SENIOR NEWS

The growth of gray-tops made the Maturity News Service
almost inevitable. It took the giant AARP to underwrite it and
make it something of a phenomenon — an exciting new experiment in American journalism.

Five veteran journalists have found a welcome home here as
well as several compatriots who report feature news about and
by seniors to more than 200 client papers.

During the next decade, the number of people over the age
of fifty is expected to grow twice as fast as the rest of the population. Gwen Gibson and Joe Volz are two reporters in their sixties who will cover this phenomenon and the interests of
retirement-age readers.

MNS reporter Gibson covers the performing arts out of the
Washington, D.C. office in the National Press Building. She used
to be on the *New York Daily News* in younger years, but instead
of remaining in retirement after years in Gotham, recycled herself
to continue her profession with the senior-oriented organization.

Joe Volz, 64, another *New York Daily News* alumnus,
became a general reporter for the MNS network. He covers
everything that is interesting and exciting about his mature audience. "I feel like a rookie reporter starting a new career," he
states with renewed enthusiasm.

## WHILE THERE'S LIFE, THERE'S OPPORTUNITY

Elderly folks well into their fifties and ranging up into the nineties have become entrepreneurs and have continued creative and highly skilled jobs from New York to Nome. Age is rarely a limiting factor. Imagination is always in fashion. Motivation is ever present, regardless of the calendar.

We picked up some old copies of *Modern Maturity* from a dozen years ago. Was it different then? Take a look:

Wilfred A. Peterson virtually invented the Art of Creative Aging. At age 77, he completed his seventh book in an Art of Living series, having sold a million copies of his books.

Pauline Lindstrom was a church activist in Grand Rapids, Michigan, who took on the job of creating a home for the elderly of her congregation. She called it Pilgrim Manor and her tireless efforts at organizing and fund-raising finally made her dream come true. When her husband died, she moved into the home herself, and continued to be its informal social director and spark plug — even until past her 90th birthday.

Another ninety-year-old was Ethel Wells Smalley of Chicago. She retired the first time from her lifetime job of being secretary to Dr. Preston Bradley, founder and pastor, till the age of 89, of the People's Church of Chicago. Miss Smalley moved to Vermont at age 85 and became secretary to the famed Maria August Trapp, a job she still held five years later.

A city of New York teacher of mathematics retired after fifty years of service in Gotham's public schools. He "retired" to become the accountant for the Association of the Blind. For off-times, he took cruises everywhere and used to tell stories to shipboard friends. "Being useful," he said, "keeps me youthful. Any day you can walk on your two legs is a good day." His name was Harold Siegal and he loved people.

In St. Petersburg, Florida, the city that has perhaps the highest percentage of retired folks, stands a library that was the brainchild and result of Thomas Dreier's efforts. It was dedicated to him when he was ninety years of age. He lived another two years to see his efforts become a very valuable and beloved resource of his adopted community. His words, which survived him, are worth recording, and we have set them down here.

"...every day is a golden day in your lives. Every day brings its gifts of goodness. Over and over again, people with whom you have had contact offer thanks to you and for you. They do this because you share your goodness with them. You do not go about toting heavy bricks of gold. Your wealth is in your thoughts and your emotions. You have made gifts as the sun makes its gifts — quietly, easily, smoothly, without apparent effort. The one word, goodness, is your magic word. Your waking hours are hours of sharing."

*–Thomas Dreier*

In the Seventies, a distinctive and pleasant voice could be heard over radio station KCRW in Santa Monica, California. It was the voice of Ruth Mills, who became ninety early in 1979. With half a century of broadcasting behind her back East, she continued for a second round on the sunnier West Coast. Her program, "The Art of Being Your Age", was heard throughout most of the 1970s every Monday afternoon without fail.

Another long-term West Coast resident was Roger Nash Baldwin. Those who knew or knew of this lawyer, remembered him as the founder of the American Civil Liberties Union, shortly after World War I. At age 94, six decades after his first commitment to Americans' civil liberties, Baldwin stated, "The ACLU... is always defending unpopular causes...but we haven't had a chance to quit." And neither did he. President Jimmy Carter awarded lawyer Baldwin the American Medal of Freedom in 1981, shortly before his demise at 97. He spanned almost a century of being an attorney, university professor, and unflinching defender of the rights of the common man.

In Glendale, California, an idea was born a score of years ago that was the brainchild of the retired director of Junior Achievement, C.W. Mike Parker. He, at 71, was not satisfied to vegetate on his former glories. So he applied what he knew best — how to motivate school youngsters to become capitalists — and started Senior Achievement. The principal purpose was to form a New Career Opportunities course that would help retirees to un-retire. With the help of June Paulson, the course developed until an average of fourty seniors, many of them couples, attended the stimulating learning and brainstorming sessions. Parker never believed in sitting in his rocking chair. "If you sit there too long," he advises, "you become part of the chair."

The intricate trail system in New Jersey's Rampos Mountains was planned in the Seventies on 2,335 acres of rocky hillsides and forest lands. The state rangers needed a man to do it: Frank Oliver, a retired engineer and editor, was called in. What was unusual about this job offer was that it was made to a man who was then 78 years young. With compass, maps, iridescent marking tape, and indomitable will power, this septuagenarian laid out the trails in a pattern that proved ideal — providing the most scenic views and the least arduous grades.

Carl Brown, a Dearborn, Michigan engineer, retired at seventy in 1965. Somewhere back in his career, Brown worked on the old Keeweenaw Central Railroad, running steam engines. It was not only a job but a blossoming love affair. He picked it up again, making his old vocation into an avocation, when he operated as engineer and sightseeing guide on the area's two antique locomotives. The Torch Lake Locomotive is the same one Brown ran as a twenty-year-old youth, except now, instead of ore and lumber, he hauls tourists…still chugging along and loving every minute of it.

Second careerists abound everywhere. All it takes is the imagination and motivations. Many of them have taken hobbies or avocations and, upon retirement, turned them into part-time vocations. Many of these new "careers" have become surprisingly successful in both satisfaction and income-production. Here are just a half dozen examples:

Vernon Hemingway, former electrical worker, also liked wood-working. In his spare time, he designed and built a prototype "Book Nook" that had display space on all four sides and wheels for mobility. He joined with his wife to sell these custom-made utility bookcases to pre-schools and children's libraries.

Cecil Moore retired from an aircraft manufacturing company. He, too, did beautiful woodwork in his spare time. Upon leaving his company, he set out to make exquisite doll houses in earnest. He now sells them to retail and toy wholesale companies, and enjoys the creativity and the income this avocation-turned-vocation provides.

George Campbell was a civil engineer in his working life, and continued his profession, but as a designer and builder of high-speed, radio-controlled toy racing boats. His designs were so successful that a Japanese manufacturer, who had seen Campbell's creations at a show, acquired a license to build them — and thus launched the retired engineer into a second career.

A "graduate" of the Parker-Paulson New Career Opportunities course described before, Gladys Lawless took her newly acquired inspiration to become agent for her late husband's religious paintings. She engaged a printer and a framer to reproduce and professionally frame the icon-like paintings and has acquired a California distributor to take her new products nationwide.

Patricia W. Bridgers changed from housekeeper to tour service operator, working out of Los Angeles. She prepared herself by taking a travel course. Following this indoctrination, she decided to specialize in the areas of her personal interest — animals, unique fashions, and special destinations. Enough travelers, evidently, shared Mrs. Bridgers' interests to create an interesting and remunerative niche for this second careerist.

Pete Damas was 73 when he decided to go into the mail order business. He was interested in plastic lamination and in collectibles, like medals that can be purchased in almost any pawn or second-hand shop. He also made up custom laminates, such as trays or pictures, that contained customers' photos and personal mementos.

Taking a plastic repair course in order to fix a turn sofa at home, Dorothy Krupp did not stop — but took the Parker-Paulson small business workshop we described previously. Combining the two skills, Mrs. Krupp was able to generate all the business she wants to handle. "I'm doing more than OK," she admits. Age is obviously no barrier to almost any business a retiree wants to launch.

# 47, 55, 56, 61, 71—
## THESE ARE BOATBUILDERS?

Port Arthur, Texas is a town where some mighty fine recreational sailboats are being built. Unfortunately, the bottom has fallen out of the recreational boat market. That, however, did not faze Al Brooks, a U.S. Naval Academy graduate who was also a math teacher, a designer, and an engineer. He had an idea for a more efficient and economical way of building a better boat — and to market it to waterfront recreation facilities.

There was another angle. In order to keep costs to a minimum, he decided to hire only elder workers who had deep reservoirs of skills, though not necessarily in boat building. He discussed his plans with a local county government placement specialist — who then came up with the personnel. The supervisor was 55; a woman welder was only 56. One laborer-turned-carpet installer and general handy-andy was a youngster of 47, while two other men, one a former sheet-metal worker, the other a former painter-carpenter, were 61 and 71. The team went to work with Al Brooks' design and motivating faith.

Supervised by the veteran boat builder, the team built the sleek, cat-rigged ketch from stem to stern and it was soon launched in the Sabine River to the applause of a sizable audience. Al Brooks confirms his faith in his crew: "These (mature workers) have a depth of skills that they can adapt to new techniques and exotic materials...They've done a great job. It's time to coin a new term — multi-skilled, experienced workers." One of the suppliers of materials for the project watched the crew at work and added, "Not only could they handle it, they improved upon it. We put their ideas into our instruction manual."

On future Sabine-Neches Boatyard projects, the five-person team that combines 290 years of experience, will serve as team leaders, teaching others what they know.

## FROM FINANCE TO FAST FOOD

Usually, at age 65, it is best to stick to one's profession. Wally Reid of Toronto, Ontario, thought differently. He was neither ready to retire nor had he lost his sense of adventure. Of course there were special circumstances — his son Larry had opened a franchise restaurant called T.G. Quickly BBQ that featured low-cholesterol food.

Within a couple of years the unique take-out restaurant was doing very well. It rode the crest of a new wave in fast food consumption, and expansion was the natural next step. Wally Reid also saw the potential and thought he'd try to apply his business experience to the BBQ. He arranged to buy a franchise from his son, took in his younger son Peter, and opened for business in March of 1988.

It took six months before the new food concept caught on in the new location, but then it took off. Reid's business experience saw him and his younger son through those first rough months. He is not planning to make this a lifetime career, but only to see the shop through to solid success — then turn it over to Peter.

And then? Wally Reid isn't saying, but by then he might be seventy and deserve another short retirement.

## CORPORATE SQUEEZE LAUNCHES NEW CAREER

Ric Gard had planned to stay with his electronic scale company in Pennsylvania till 65 and then take the normal retirement route to the golf course. It didn't quite work out that way. A few years before retirement, his president died and the new owners wanted to put their own people into the key slots. Gard's hand was forced. He was "retired" and for a while became a consultant for other companies.

Then a couple of years later, in mid-1988, he was introduced by a business broker to a mobile car-care business that also did lubrication and oil change on the customer's premises. It was a franchise and promised to ride a crest of popularity and potential success. Gard talked it over with his son-in-law and decided to buy the franchise.

As usual, the first few months were slow. Only twenty cars per month, on an average, were serviced. Then it started to build. After a little more than a year, volume had climbed to 750 a month. Gard takes care of the marketing end, and his son-in-law takes care of operations. It is a good symbiosis, both using their strengths to the advantage of the business.

He figures it will take a while longer before his son-in-law is able to take over the marketing and management functions as well. And then? "Then," says Ric Gard, "I'll retire to the good life." Maybe. Meanwhile, he is happily busy and making money.

## LIFE CONTINUES AT 93

One wintry day in 1985, a crowd of Gray Panthers were joined by school children one-sixth their age. All were carrying placards proclaiming, "Don't Discriminate on the Basis of Age," and they marched up and down peacefully in front of the State House in Boston, Massachusetts. This protest didn't just happen. It was orchestrated by none other than Edward L. Bernays, the father of modern public relations.

This in itself would be a noteworthy event, but certainly not earth-shaking. What made it unique, however, was that the organizer, Bernays, was then 93 years old. He was co-chairman of the Committee for Economic Justice for Older Workers in Cambridge, MA; honorary chairman of Careers for Later Years, a group that helps older workers find jobs; and chairman of a citizens' advisory committee to the Massachusetts State Department of Elder Affairs.

Bernays, of course, is not your ordinary senior citizen. He virtually invented modern public relations in America during World War I, when he helped President Woodrow Wilson prepare the nation for its war with Germany. He was the nephew of Dr. Sigmund Freud, and a friend of such youngsters as Congressman Claude Pepper, Bob Hope, and Anthony Quinn.

Obviously more active than men thirty years younger, Bernays was quoted as saying, "I hate the word 'retirement'. It used to suggest a certain dignity, but today means only that the guy is old and decrepit and can't work any longer."

## BURIED ALIVE

This is a business? It is for Dr. Roy Wolford, 67, and his crew of scientists, who inhabit Biosphere II in the Sonora Desert outside of Tucson, Arizona. Walford is chief of medical operations on the eight-man crew that is testing out life in an ideal world of 2½ acres — lush gardens of tropical plants, supersize vegetables, a man-made tidal sea, and a large variety of scientific and agricultural gadgetry.

The purpose of this life-size experiment is to test a self-sustaining colony as it might be erected in a space platform or on another planet. Just in case, under the huge dome, the Biosphere

II capsule will be Dr. Wolford's and his cohorts' home for two years from September 26, 1991 to September 25, 1993.

When Dr. Wolford comes out of the capsule, he will be nearly seventy. Will he then retire? "No way," he confirms. "I'll be ready for another career. Probably writing." We hope to be waiting to read his report.

# Retire From Your Job, But Not From Work

*Work for the good of your self-esteem. Work to get some structure in your life. Work for the fun of working. Work to get out of your spouse's hair. Work to satisfy your survival instinct and your work ethic. Work for any or all of the above reasons, but* work!

—Howard Shank

in *Managing Retirement*
(Contemporary Books, 1985)

# CHAPTER VII

## TO PROMOTE YOUR BUSINESS OR YOURSELF

To start a business or to get back into the job market, you need to know how to promote the most important package: YOU.

If you were working for a large company before, or were in a civil service or military agency, blending in with the crowd and not making waves was more of a norm than turning a spotlight on yourself. Not so once you start looking for a new salaried or commissioned slot; even less so if you venture out into the competitive land of Entrepreneurs.

In other words, your public *image* determines how you can blow your horn and how effective it will be in the perception of the people you are trying to influence. Everything but everything affects this image. The two dozen facets of your "horn blowing melody" are a fairly good start, though there indubitably are others.

Surveys have been conducted among companies that have gone bankrupt to determine why some go belly up and others, in very similar circumstances, are able to survive. One principal reason always stands out: company image or reputation.

A business that has a good reputation, whose credibility is high, whose products are known for their honesty and whose service can be relied upon often survives downturns and problems that sink organizations with lesser qualities.

Few images were more exciting, few words more dramatic, than those of President John F. Kennedy. Had it not been that public perception was so idealistic, our young president would possibly have faced censure if not impeachment proceedings. The same might be said about President Franklin Delano Roosevelt, or even about some of our Founding Fathers.

The ways to blow your horn are sometimes called promotions or public relations. These activities can include any or all of the following functions, and possibly many more:

- Business stationery
- The way you dress
- The organizations you belong to
- How you network yourself
- Your car or delivery vehicles
- How your employees are trained
- The kind of letters you send out
- What ads you run in the media
- How your phone is answered
- How you follow up on sales or services
- The quality of your goods and service
- The packaging of your products
- The signs on your property
- How others describe you, particularly publications
- How you and yours behave in public
- How thoughtful you are on special occasions
- Where you take your vacations, travel or recreation
- The books and journals you read and refer to
- Your speech pattern and vocabulary
- Your educational credentials
- The furnishing of your business location
- How promptly you pay your bills
- What credibility your public statements have
- And finally, what the public says about you and your business, its products and services

Going into business, or going back into the job market, requires an understanding of these *image* forces. Blowing your horn sweetly can overcome many adverse circumstances, such as age. Playing the right tune can expedite financing, start-up time, and costs, and, in the case of workforce re-entry, open doors magically.

Let's take a look at the 24 steps or check-points that have been suggested as being important to your entrepreneurial horn-blowing. It's sort of a piece of sheet music by which you can play your way into a business or into a job.

*Letterhead:* In any kind of business or work situation, some form of correspondence will become necessary. An exploratory inquiry, a follow-up thank you note, an explanation of your services or products, a fill-in of matters unsaid during your face-to-face encounter, a cover memo to accompany various enclosures, etc. ...all of these require some form of communication, whether by post, messenger, or fax. You cannot always make this contact in person, hence your letterhead becomes your ambassador — and the impression it makes, the image of you and your product/ service it evokes, can be the determining factor between "sale" or "no sale". Good stationery is expensive these days, but even at 15¢ to 40¢ each, your letter becomes the one most important messenger in your business or personal arsenal.

*Dress:* The story of Howard Hughes' dress code is well-known. But then if you are an eccentric billionaire, you can indulge in unusual behavior and dress. For most of us ordinary mortals, the way we present ourselves to a prospective customer, client or employer, a financier or important supplier, sets the tone for all future relationships. Ask yourself before you set forth, "What kind of impression do I want to create?" You want to look confident, perhaps even successful and prosperous, in tune with the business situation — and yet, you don't want to make your opposite feel uncomfortable or show him up or appear superior. Sometimes the very tie you choose, or the way your shoes are shined, will indicate whether you are conservative, orderly, efficient — or careless. If you want to put your best foot forward, make sure it is well shined, said one advisor, while another added that you don't have to be a millionaire to dress like one.

*Organizations:* Belonging to the right organizations accomplishes two important functions for a business person or job seeker — it says who you are and with whom you keep company, and it allows you to network, which is still the best way to make contacts and get ahead. For retirees going back into business, especially if this is in another location, membership in organizations such as the local chamber of commerce is eminently worthwhile. Other memberships to consider are the Better Business Bureau, a board of trade, a business or professional society in your field, and a civic or service club composed of like-minded individuals. If you are married, your wife's memberships can also be valuable, especially if mixed functions take place occasionally. One consultant formed a breakfast club in his town. Up to two dozen business and professional men and women meet each Tuesday morning in a local hotel restaurant to exchange experiences, business cards, and leads to local businesses that have just started or remodeled or are known to have particular needs.

*Networking:* Where you are seen and with whom can be important to getting leads to new business and contacts. It could be an organization, popular restaurant, civic or political function, weekly civic or service club luncheon, country club, professional society, or a membership meeting of a non-profit group. The paragraph *Organizations,* above, goes into more detail on this point. Many entrepreneurs have told about the importance of networking, especially in getting a job at this age, or making contacts for professional services — giving networking a two- or three-to-one advantage over advertising.

*Vehicles:* Wouldn't you agree that it can make different impressions on others whether you drive up in a rakish sportscar, an elegant import limousine, a ten-year-old Chevy, or a panel truck? Like your personal dress, the kind of car you drive to work and the manner in which you maintain that car will make varying impact on your business associates. If your business uses a delivery or company vehicle, it should always reflect favorably on your company and product — being clean and operating efficiently, and lettered with an appropriate but effective message. That vehicle, after all, can be considered a mobile billboard for your business. Why not take advantage of the potential impact?

*Employee training:* Inside or outside, the people who work for you are your representatives. Often the only difference between a $5 meal and a $15 meal is the way it is served. The clerk who is polite and informative can bring a customer or client back more assuredly than all the costly promotional efforts. Conversely, a rude, ill-dressed, badly spoken person behind the desk or counter can negate the most sophisticated and expensive advertising and public relations efforts. Employees invariably do not have the same attitude as managers and bosses. If they did, they probably would own the business — or soon could. If you are hiring any employees, no matter on what level, you need to include in the hiring process a system for training — and not just a one-time shot, but a continuous training effort that will render both awards and demerits. An employees' handbook that spells out your policy in great detail, even if this is only a two-pager, is a virtual necessity, guaranteed to repay you in many ways.

*Letter-writing:* (See previous entry for *Letterheads.*) Your best designed and printed stationery will be so much waste paper if the message it carries is inappropriate, sloppy, or untimely. Letter-writing is something of an art, though it is no mystery. A business letter, written for whatever reason, even on your personal behalf, is nothing more than a personal message that utilizes the typed or word processed medium. The letter should reflect the way you talk. In addition to neatness and professional format (which ought to be obvious), a business letter should be (1) pertinent, to-the-point and complete in its presentation or reply, and (2) sent without delay, if it is in answer to an inquiry or order. The sad fact is that, in our experience, business correspondence is one of the most neglected forms of communication. It is slowly becoming the dinosaur of business contacts, being squeezed out by more convenient electronic media that will rarely, however, transmit the personality and feeling of a thoughtful business letter.

*Advertising:* Ads are also a reflection of your business and product image. The layout or design, the amount of white space, the type style or typography, the kind of illustration, and the wording or copy all harmonize to effect an image and create the desired results for the sponsor — or become eminently forgettable or skippable. It costs the same to publish a good ad as a lousy ad. Either one costs a great deal of money. You might as well get the biggest bang for your buck. If you have any doubt about creating the right kind of image with your ad, get a professional to help you, and that includes selecting the right media that reaches the right kind of people. More money is wasted on ineffective media choices than on any other facet of advertising.

*Phone Answering:* More and more business is conducted by telephone. It is almost becoming too hectic to venture on some streets and too costly to make personal calls. For these and many other reasons, answering a telephone is a vital function of any business. Often it is the only contact. Even in making an appointment, whether for a sales presentation or a job interview, the phone contact can determine whether you will even get a second chance. If you have employees, all of them should be adequately trained in answering your phone uniformly, warmly, agreeably. If phone calls become too frequent, install another line. Our own opinion is that an additional line or number is a good investment and much preferable to "call waiting" — which can be most annoying and impolite.

*Follow-Up:* Whether you will make a product sale or a service call, such a contact provides an opening for a second and third sale. Businesses consider a customer or client who has bought something many times more valuable than a "cold" prospect. When you consider the value of a real live customer or client, and the impact he or she has on new contacts, then the need for a prompt follow-up of some kind becomes more obvious. Preferred follow-ups are usually a written or printed thank you note, a word of appreciation, or even a follow-up enclosure describing or picturing additional offerings. Important: Follow-up quickly while you, your product, or service are fresh in the mind of the customer or client.

*Quality:* This is the quintessence of business. As one writer put it: If you can't do it right the first time, will you have time to do it over again? Quality is a physical thing, but it starts in the mind. If you operate a one-person business, then *you* can control every step of the production of your product or service. If, however, you have employees, getting them to become quality-conscious will require considerable training and perpetual motivation. Quality and quality control become even more important if you do repeat business with the same customers or clients, if you depend on networking, or if you sell premium goods at higher prices.

*Packaging:* Proper packaging serves several purposes — protection of a product, messages that offer instruction-for-use, identification of product and company, and to establish an image or aura for the product. Sometimes the package is used to promote the product, as a dispenser, or even as a display. A luxury product that is sold at a high price and/or high mark-up, demands an attractive package that says, "I'm worth the price" or "This prestigious product is worth what I'm asking". Perfume, for example, can come in packages that cost several dollars, but they are the magnets that attract shoppers to the product and no question is asked of the lofty price tag. Convenience foods come in plastic packages that display the product as well as protect it, and are either easy to open, serve as cooking utensils, or can be re-used. Many packages today are designed for either recycling or biodegradability — and this environmental impact on packaging is an important factor as we move toward the new millennium of ecology-consciousness.

*Signs:* If you are opening a business that requires sign identification, make sure that the kind of sign you have in mind can indeed be installed. Zoning and lease restrictions might weigh against your preconceived sign design. Look most of all for visibility. Many a great-looking design appears wonderful on the drawing board, but becomes illegible from a distance, or blends totally into the background, or fights surrounding signs into oblivion. Look also for maintenance problems. Some signs are easily harmed by storms or vandals; others require illumination to be seen at a distance, at dawn or dusk, or demand costly service contracts. If you expect customers, clients, deliverymen and others to come to your premises, make sure your building or house number can be read easily — even at night.

*Others' Image:* Sticks and stones may not break your bones, but words can truly hurt you. What do people say about you and your business? How are you and your enterprise mentioned in the local media? Do they talk about you — favorably? Re-read the beginning of this section to determine what makes for a *reputation* and then work on building yours through all the facets we described — with emphasis on favorable publicity that you send out regularly to all local or trade media.

*Public Behavior:* While you can get lost in the anonymity of a huge city, doing business in a small town or suburb requires the establishment of a sterling reputation in personal as well as professional conduct. Loose lips can sink our ships, they used to say during World War II. They can also scuttle a business if bad behavior in public, by you or yours, spotlights your feet of clay.

*Thoughtfulness:* A large and often unspectacular aspect of good public relations comes from your personal, one-on-one thoughtfulness. This characteristic is not easily learned. It is usually a part of our behavior pattern; a part of our upbringing. But it can, to a large degree, be acquired and taught. Mostly, it can become a part of company policy. Examples: Always saying "Thank you" or "I really appreciate this" to a customer or client; sending a little thank you note after a luncheon, a function, or a purchase by the customer/client; remembering an important occasion, like a birthday or anniversary; following up a purchase with an inquiry as to the customer's/client's satisfaction; offering a little trinket to an accompanying child or to the receptionist; remembering to inquire about the children or spouse or parent.

*Vacation Destination:* There is a certain snob appeal to telling your customers/clients about your cruise or vacation in the islands. Being seen in prestigious places and letting impressions and names drop occasionally might sound snobby, but it does impress many people — and it makes you such an interesting conversationalist. Often attendance at a business conference or convention can be combined with networking — and reduce the cost by taking a legitimate tax deduction. Good planning of such recreational-cum-business events can pay off twice.

*Reading:* Your reading list of magazines and journals, the daily and Monday morning business sections, provide a continuing source of education. For decades I have clipped articles of interest to me and filed them. It has saved me many trips to the library, enabled me to spark conversations, and updated my knowledge about events and businesses, people and place. The annual cost of subscriptions and newsstand purchases is probably under $200, about the price of a low-budget seminar or college course.

*Speech:* Your communication skills tell a lot about you and your business or profession. It is easy to downgrade your vocabulary, but virtually impossible to upgrade it, should the occasion demand, if you do not have a reservoir of words. Two handy sources in my regular intellectual pantry for building a vocabulary are the monthly word list in the *Reader's Digest* and doing the daily crossword puzzle in the newspaper, and/or other word games that happen to emerge from the day's reading. The English language is the greatest repository of vocabulary in the world, drawing on German, Scandinavian, French, Latin, Greek, and even Hebrew, Swahili, Indian (both American and Hindu), and many other tongues that have come into contact with the ubiquitous American. It becomes a game, a habit, to add words to your intellectual storehouse; few addictions could be as useful and beneficial as this.

*Education:* There is some dissent about the need for education in entrepreneurship. Those who have made it by their bootstraps might decry the achievement of the MBA or PhD whose D&B is far lower. As a general rule, I would disagree. Education not only exposes the student to knowledge, but gives the mind an opportunity for gestation of information. It is a lifetime occupation and should never stop as long as eyes and mind remain open.

*Decorating:* The furnishing of your business location says much about you. Even if you work, or are planning to work, from home, your physical environment should be comfortable, productive, and impressive if you have customers or clients visit you. Like the attire of your body, the furnishing of your work environment says much about it. It tells of efficiency, success — or the lack of them. Furnishings can, and often have, become an albatross and an invitation to bankruptcy. Many a would-be success has started out with meager capital and little business but tons of decorating opulence. When the cash flow that was erroneously anticipated did not materialize, the capital invested up-front in costly trimmings became the catalyst to failure. Would it not be better to grow gradually into showroom excellence? Or lease furniture rather than buy it, during the formative start-up period? Today's need for expensive machinery is also a cause for concern, especially since computers, fax, and copy machines, communications equipment and all the trappings of an office of the 1990s are subject to annual obsolescence. Check with your accountant to ascertain whether you are better off leasing such equipment, rather than spending working capital that might be impossible to obtain, if necessary, from normal financing sources.

*Bill Payment:* Ever since the debacle of an early start-up more than 25 years ago, I have been gun-shy of debts. I have never, to my recollection, paid a late-payment fee or penalty. My credit card company keeps upgrading my credit and I can look any vendor in the eye knowing I do not owe him a cent. I sleep better at night and never need to borrow, except for major acquisitions, such as a house. Your vendors, suppliers, customers, clients, friends, and family will know you by the credit you keep.

*Public Statements:* If you are, ever have been, or will be, in a position to be quoted in a newspaper or magazine article, or give a talk at a civic or professional meeting, you want to be sure your comments are credible. What you say in public becomes part of your image. It can make or break your reputation. Assuming, therefore, that you know your business and don't mind airing your views for the record, such exposure is invaluable. In fact, it is a function you should pursue assiduously. Even a letter-to-the-editor can have a favorable public impact. An article written for a professional journal, with your by-line and identification appended, is more valuable than a paid full-page ad. An interesting talk, punctuated by genuine information and humor, can be quoted many times by members of the audience, and even reproduced in a news medium — adding to your reputation, self-satisfaction, and success. Such occasions should even be planned and sought. Your age, in this instance (assuming you are of retirement age) can be a boon. A silver-top plus golden words often makes a valuable amalgam.

*Public Opinion:* What the public says about you, the summation of all your public relations efforts discussed in these previous pages, is the bottom line. The British poet John Donne said it four centuries ago: "No man is an island," and indeed he is not. Even the entrepreneur, the supposedly solitary rock of self-sufficiency and confidence, must work within a society of peers and lesser lights. The quality of your product and service, the performance of your promise, the credibility of your word — they all work together to create that ephemeral commodity, success. And if this then should be your Retirement Career, time is not infinite. You can use all the help you can get. Public opinion is one.

## MARKETING TO OTHER SENIORS

While it is not necessary that retirees going back to work or into business selling to and servicing other seniors exclusively, it is more than likely that peers and peer groups will be among the primary prospects. Selling to seniors is not so easy, simply because so many mistakes are being made in present-day marketing methods. Even as seniors ourselves, it is all too true that we do not always know ourselves.

The 55-year-old-and-over group, as an important consumer segment, has become the single richest category of purchasers in America. It stands to reason that marketeers and researchers have studied and are continuing to study this group to see what makes them tick and how they can be milked to generate more money.

Georgia State University's Center for Mature Consumer Studies conducted a survey among 1,000 older consumers, across the nation. Eighty percent of them expressed their dissatisfaction with the way companies are marketing their products and services to them. Seventy percent were strong on stating that packages and bottles were difficult to open. Sixty percent said that the type on product and instruction labels was too small to read comfortably.

This over-55-year-old group comprises only 23% of our current population, but controls 75% of the nation's wealth and about 50% of its discretionary income. You can bet your bottom dollar that marketers are going to pay attention to these figures, and if you join them with a business of your own, you can benefit by knowing yourself and your peers.

As mature entrepreneurs, we must make sure that we are not caught in the trap that so many younger business people fall into — and that is to stereotype seniors.

One of the greatest transgressions in either stereotyping or ignoring the richest single consumer group — and that is *us* — takes place in the advertisements in print and on the air. Not everyone over 55 years of age is old and sickly, inactive and strapped, stingy and crotchety. The over-55ers come in all shapes and sizes and proclivities. They just might spend their money a little more carefully, a little differently.

---

## TO HELP BLOW YOUR OWN HORN, HERE'S WHAT'S AVAILABLE IN RETIREMENT PLANNING

All over the country, programs are offered at area colleges, community colleges, state and federal offices, private seminars, and senior organizations such as the AARP. Also check with the local libraries for programs within the system or for any others known to them. These are typical of such programs offered in the Washington, D.C. area:

- Three-day seminar at the Department of Agriculture
- One-day workshop, New Look at Retirement, at Georgetown University
- Retirement Planning, a full-semester course at Montgomery County, Maryland Public Schools, Adult Education Division
- Retirement Planning, a two-hour course given day and evening, at Northern Virginia Community College
- Retirement Income, a two-session course at Northern Virginia Community College, evening session
- Financial Planning to Fight Inflation, at above school
- Design for Leisure, a course in creative retirement living, at University of Virginia, Falls Church campus
- Retirement Planning, the Newest Employee Benefit course at Georgetown University for personnel administrators (two days)
- AARP guide books and pamphlets available free or at small charge

The Georgia State study indicated that these senior consumers — there are about 57 million of them — can be divided into four distinct consumer groups. It is good for us to know them, no matter which one you might fall into:

1. *"Healthy Hermits"* (38%) — can be reached most effectively through direct mail and print media; good market for tax and legal advice, do-it-yourself products, home entertainment, domestic services.
2. *"Ailing Outgoers"* (34%) — responsive to group sales of various related products at one time, sales promotions, and special services; good market for planned communities, medical and health services, health products, leisure activities.
3. *"Frail Recluses"* (15%) — best reached through mass media or group product sales (cross selling); good market for home health care products, medical services, home entertainment.
4. *"Healthy Indulgers"* (13%) — the smallest but most viable group for "second careerists" and marketers in general. This target group adds up to more than seven million potential customers. Best way to reach them is with in-store promotions, direct mail, targeted print media; good market for financial services, travel, entertainment, clothing, high-tech products.

It is evident that to reach older consumers, one cannot lump them into age categories. Attitudes are a more valid and more accurate criterion of consumer reaction. The marketing task of reaching older consumers, therefore, is a two-step process:

- Identifying and understanding the different types of older consumers,

- Persuading them to divest themselves of their fears, phobias — and money.

## YOUR JOB SEARCH ASSETS AFTER AGE 50

The AARP, The American Association for Retired Persons, has a booklet available for mature individuals who want to go back to work, rather than attempting to start a business of their own. It is called *"Working Options: How to Plan Your Job Search,*

*Your Work Life.*" Request a free copy of this excellent booklet by asking for number PW (1090) D 12303 and mail it to AARP Fulfillment, 1909 K St., NW, Washington, DC 20049.

In addition to telling you how to search for a job and create a productive resume, it offers a number of statements that you may want to use. They are positive statements that make good copy for cover letters and give mature job-seekers the power-boost for faltering egos. For instance:

Older workers

- ... have work experience that has given them specialized knowledge and skills.
- ... measure up — productivity is as high in most jobs as other age groups.
- ... care about the quality of their work; they are loyal, dedicated, reliable employees.
- ... often want to continue working — retirement is only one option.
- ... bring mature judgement, good basic skills, and experience with people to the job.
- ... have proven that they can adapt to the job and to change — in family, the work, and the world.
- ... have fewer accidents on the job than other groups.
- ... have attendance records are equal to or better than most age groups.
- ... are capable decision-makers and problem solvers.
- ... health and benefit costs are the same or lower than other age groups.
- ... often stay longer on the job, on an average, than younger employees.

In summation, employers are looking for qualities that many older workers possess, such as:

- Low turnover, reducing need for training of new employees
- Less absenteeism
- Good basic skills
- Conscientiousness and industriousness
- Loyalty to the company or organization

- Ability to get along well with other co-workers and customers
- Flexibility and grace under pressure.

The AARP reports that it takes the average worker age 55 or more an average of 10.5 weeks to be relocated. If at that age you do not wish to, or cannot afford to, retire, then the "selling points" above can help you speed up the in-between process. Use them to "blow your horn" for yourself and your peers.

Another AARP spokesman adds some good advice. When you write a resume for yourself, and it sounds like you might be blowing your horn too loudly, put a mute in your resume — skip some of the nitty-gritty details and punctuate the highlights. Put yourself in the shoes of the 35-year-old interviewer who is awestruck by your stellar list of achievements. He might have a $25,000 job available, but he is staring at a $50,000 list. How can he offer you such a low-paying position? Would he insult you? So he might say, "Your qualifications are superb, but you are very much overqualified for this job." You will have a hard time answering that one — but it is possible. You might want to assure him that —

"Frankly, I am not on a career track — I just want to work, and am looking for a place where I can use my experience and expertise to benefit others."

Another AARP advisor pointed out that the mid-level executive who lost his job in one company, is still too viable to retire, and wants to go back to work — at least for a few years — needs to take a revised attitude toward his next position. "Now is the time," she said, "to look at what you really want from a job. What's more important to you? Do you need to work with people? Travel? Work close to home? Don't look for the next step up the career ladder (as you did some years ago) — look for a job where you'll be the happiest." And let your next interviewer know about it.

**Try not to be desperate. This kind of attitude comes through very negatively.** It can be the kiss of death in an interview. Take heart, instead, on what Marion Jacknow of Fairfax, Virginia's Program for Mature Workers advised: "There's never been a better time than this to be an older worker. More and more employers are starting to realize that seniors make terrific employees."

## HIRING THE OVER-65S

Demographic predictions by the Council of Governments are that the younger population will decline, while those 65 or over will increase substantially. After 2005, the population over 65 will increase even more rapidly. Some companies are already noting this trend and are tapping the older work force.

Giant Foods of Landover, Maryland, is making special efforts to attract older workers back to the corporate fold.

Marriott Corporation's work force already stands at 14% of all employees who are over 55. Between now and 1995, about 20% of vacancies will occur and older workers are being eyed for many positions.

Roy Rogers/Hardy employs 250 older people as hosts, cashiers, and maintenance people, and the list is growing.

---

### LAUREN BACALL

The famous movie star, Lauren Bacall, was asked a few years ago why she was still working. She replied, "I really hate it when people say to me, 'Are you still working?' Am I still *walking? Breathing?* Who decided you're supposed to stop at a certain point? I've worked all my life. Why should I stop now? What else would I do?" Ms. Bacall celebrates her 68th birthday this year.

---

## HOW WOMEN CAN MAKE THE MOST OF IT

Women are in a special category. Some of them "retire" at age 23 — to marry and raise a family. Then they want to rejoin the workforce at, let's say, age 40 or 42, or start a business of their own or with a woman-partner. The motivation might be ambition, financial need, divorce, widowhood, or simply boredom. There's just one problem: lack of experience.

Women who "retire" at the end of the traditional work-life, let's say at age sixty or sixty-five, are unlikely to rejoin the ranks of employees or entrepreneurs. There are exceptions, of course, and as more and more women ascend the ranks of professionals and corporate managers, the higher the incident of re-entry at an advanced age.

Retirement for women does not hold the same definition, then, as it might for men. It can come at almost any age from forty to sixty-five. Women, too, are prone to two problems not usually encountered as frequently by men: real or perceived age discrimination, and self-perceived aging syndrome.

Discrimination on a corporate as well as personal level is commonplace in the business world. It is, however, difficult to prove, even though it exists. Even the Equal Employment Opportunity Commission (EEOC) is spectacularly ineffective in pursuing reported cases of evident age discrimination.

One older woman receptionist in a large office was "retired" prematurely, because the department head wanted a young, pretty woman to be up front where visitors (and he himself) could be welcomed by a rosy-cheeked, unlined face. Discrimination complaints came to naught. But there is a wonderful conclusion to this story. The "retired" woman, a capable and ambitious lady of 58, went into business for herself. She used her many business contacts to line up computer work, both secretarial and accounting, with other companies that were occasionally or seasonally overloaded, and needed competent, affordable temporary assistance. Within a year, the lady began to farm out her own overload to other women who worked from home to add to their incomes.

Discrimination is often difficult to pin down. David Gamse, director of the AARP's Worker Equity Department, was quoted on this subject:

"Some people do not know the difference between part-time work and temporary full-time work. When they are let go from the latter, they often think they are being discriminated against. Some haven't kept current in their field, or don't know how to seek work effectively. And too many are ready to retire, relocate to some place such as Sun City, Arizona, then realize they would still like to work — but can't find a job. The problem is usually not age discrimination; the problem is too few jobs in Sun City for the number of people who are looking for work."

The same rationale, of course, goes for starting a business —

and we discuss this situation in the next chapter on *Relocating*.

Aging is a phase of retirement that seems to affect women more than men. The old story of "Mirror, mirror on the wall..." expresses the age-old shibboleth that older women cannot hack it in the business world. Nothing can be further from the truth. It is a male-inspired form of social discrimination that was best put down by the last actress Billie Burke, who passed away at age 85. She said, "Age is something that doesn't matter, unless you are a cheese."

In a culture that glorifies youth and beauty, older women entrepreneurs are gaining considerable ground. Fortunately, two trends come to the rescue of mature women. First, business and industry are increasingly appreciating the skill, reliability, and experience of older women and, pushed by anti-discrimination legislation, are making more and more use of the older woman's frequently superior abilities. Second, more and more older women are entering the ranks of entrepreneurship.

There is a good reason for this latter trend. Women are gaining more experience because more of them are in the workforce; more women are forced to be independent because of divorce or early deaths of their mates; and women are becoming better educated and more secure in their roles.

A good book on the subject of aging women and the beauty myth is Naomi Wolf's *"The Beauty Myth: How Images of Beauty Are Used Against Women."* Considerable inspiration can also be drawn from the pages of business magazines like *Working Woman, INC., Entrepreneur,* and *Modern Maturity,* which regularly report on mature women who enter the business world with notable success.

One aspect of female success in business is their growing resourcefulness and confidence, generated by their experience in the business and corporate world. Susan Butler of Women in Communication put her hand on one vital point: "Women need to take more risks, to venture into new directions. They have nothing to lose but their chains."

Membership in a growing number of good organizations is also germane to women's ascendancy in the business world. Such networking will help women retirees at whatever age gain confidence, as well as knowledge that might be lacking, to take that quantum jump into entrepreneurial independence. Some of the organizations available to women include:

Women's Business Opportunities, a division of the U.S. Small
Business Administration, located in the more than 100 SBA
field offices across the United States, as well as in many of
the 385 SCORE offices. See the blue government section
in metropolitan telephone books, under SBA, for the
nearest office.

National Alliance of Homebased Businesswomen (NAHB),
P.O. Box 95, Norwood, NJ 07640.

American Women's Economic Development Corporation
(AWED), 60 E. 42nd St., New York, NY 10165, (800)
222-AWED.

National Coalition for Women's Enterprise, Inc., 30 Irving Place
(9th floor), New York, NY 10003, (212) 505-2090.

International Women's Networking Business Conference
(IWNBC), 1701 K St., NW, Suite 204, Washington, DC
20006, (202) 331-2142.

American Business Women's Association, P.O. Box 8728, 9100
Ward Parkway, Kansas City, MO 64114, (816) 361-6621.

Women's Economic Development Corp., 1885 University Ave.,
West (Suite 315), St. Paul, MN 55104.

American Association of Black Women Entrepreneurs, P.O. Box
13933, Silver Spring, MD 20911-3933, (301) 565-0258.

Women Construction Owners and Executives, USA, P.O. Box
883034, San Francisco, CA 94188-3034, (415) 467-2140.

Women who are looking to relocate and start a business or go
back to work, can find considerable advice. One writer, Jill
Andresky Fraser, listed the best cities and best companies to
work for in her book *The Best U.S. Cities for Working Women,*
as follows:

*Best cities:* New York, Chicago, Los Angeles, Minneapolis/
St. Paul, San Diego, Atlanta and Dallas, followed by Boston, San
Francisco, Washington DC, Phoenix and Kansas City.

*Best corporations:* Aetna Life and Casualty, Hartford,
Connecticut; Ask Computer Systems, Los Altos, California;
Baxter Travenol Laboratories, Deerfield, Illinois; City Corp,
New York; Conde Nast Publications, New York, New York;

Control Data Corporation, Minneapolis, Minnesota; General Electric, Fairfield, Connecticut; General Mills, Minneapolis, Minnesota; IBM, Armonk, New York; and 3M, St. Paul, Minnesota.

For other comments on relocation, see the following chapter on this subject.

A comforting closing comment comes from Naomi Wolf's book, in which she states, "Older women are more energetic, more powerful, more comfortable with their abilities. They need to recognize these qualities and disentangle themselves from the beauty myth."

You can't

*help getting*

*older, but you*

*don't have to*

*get old.*

—George Burns

# CHAPTER VIII

## AMERICA'S BEST PLACES TO OPEN A BUSINESS, GET ANOTHER JOB, AND ENJOY LIFE

A tall order! But here it is: the moment for decision.

You have either been handed that Golden Parachute and "retired", or you have decided, entirely on your own, to take the plunge into entrepreneurship. Whatever your *economic* motivation, there remains this decision: If you are going to relocate, you might as well do it to a place where life is great.

Many retirees have discovered that work and making money is not all that there is to living. *Lifestyle* is important, too, especially if the years are speeding by and you have more years behind you than in front of you.

Several factors tend to keep many of us rooted to where we are:

● We have a homestead that is virtually paid off. The expenses consist of taxes and maintenance. Why move and incur higher costs elsewhere?

● Our friends and family are in the area, especially the children and grandchildren. How can we leave them?

● If we are going into business elsewhere, we won't know as many people, organizations, suppliers, or old contacts. Can we start all over again?

The older we get, the harder it will be to uproot ourselves and migrate to a new and unfamiliar location. So what's the answer?

156 CHAPTER VIII

How do we convince ourselves that the grass is indeed greener on the other side of the fence — that the pot of gold at the end of the rainbow is no fake?

Any relocation, especially at an advanced age, must have some terrific rationale. It must be preceded by considerable investigation, and that is what we are about to do.

What would get us to relocate in the first place? Let us count the ways:

1. Better weather. Age brings on an appreciation of the benefits of good weather. Younger people, particularly those with growing children, have also discovered the lure of good weather. Florida now has more than thirteen million inhabitants. Fewer than three million are retirees.

2. Improved lifestyle, including year-round access to recreation, especially outdoor activities like golf, tennis, boating, and swimming.

3. Escape from giant-city living with its attendant pollution, crowding, crime rate, traffic, and high prices.

4. A change from a cumbersome house to a one-level living facility that has built-in maintenance — preferably in a location that is more affordable.

5. A location that is close to needed amenities, such as airport, good medical service, convenient shopping.

If relocation involves going into business, then a number of economic factors need to be considered as well.

1. Are your skills needed in the area? Do you have helpful contacts and connections? Can they be developed easily? Is it a growth area where business can find a niche?

2. What networking opportunities are available? What information is available on local economic conditions? What help? Are the local folks receptive, helpful, friendly?

3. What kind of infrastructure is available? Is the government user-friendly toward newcomers? Is the tax structure comfortable? Is zoning appropriate for what I require?

4. Are suppliers nearby? Is there a labor pool to draw from if I need help? What are the going salary rates?
5. What are rentals like? Competition? Income levels? Costs for housing, food and services? Insurance rates and utility costs? Transportation? Sales tax?

Other relocation considerations might revolve around cultural amenities, such as schools, universities, libraries, museums, and theaters. It all depends on your penchant for what *you* need. The list is endless. Until...you make numerous trips to the intended relocation area, until you have, preferably, tried living there for a while, it will be difficult to assess such a move objectively. Possibly even more difficult to assess are the subjective reasons that provide often insurmountable hurdles — especially to a female member of the team — and these include children, close friends, relatives, and a homestead of long standing, not to mention the familiarity of the streets, the local supermarket, and all those nice little stores where the missus has been trading for many years.

What makes a professional or commercial relocation easier is to satisfy the *personal hurdles* first. Here are two ways this might be accomplished:

• Make a list of all the factors that you and your spouse want in the ideal location: weather, security, affordability, health care, convenient transportation, desirable housing, recreational and cultural amenities, other family members or close friends nearby, reasonable tax and inheritance laws.

• Make a second list of all communities that come close to offering most of the above facilities. Be prepared to do some compromising. Even Eden was not perfect; it had snakes.

Now make a list of what you want professionally or in a business. It is possible, and even likely, that you will need to reverse this process of rationalization. If the right economic opportunity arises in a location that is not perfect from a personal standpoint, then you will have to do some concerted compromising. However, consider that if you are of retirement age and you do have some dependable income, your personal desires should precede the commercial or professional mandates.

At this age, presuming again that you are around retirement

age, don't you deserve to be happy? To enjoy life? If you agree, then you will want to put the proper emphasis on the ingredients of your decision. Remember, that a drastic move of this kind becomes harder and harder as you grow older. Pre-planning all details is not only cost-effective and more efficient, it is absolutely essential for your physical and emotional life. Even more so for that of your spouse.

When considering the commercial or professional possibilities of a new location, much depends on what you plan to do once you get there, and what type of enterprise or profession you wish to entertain.

If you are going to buy somebody else's business, join a previously established business, or buy a franchise that is preplanned to be in that location, then the choices have already been made for you.

Should you, on the other hand, be uncommitted to the kind of enterprise you want to undertake, but set on the location for sundry personal reasons, then you will want to pursue two other avenues:

- Establish a residence in the new location and start "looking around" — doing your own eye-ball research by visiting neighborhoods and talking to the locals; peruse the local media for business and professional leads, talk to one or more business brokers, or visit the chamber of commerce and attend some luncheon meetings of a civic or service club;

- Go to work, even part-time, in a related business, to get the feel of the local economy and to pick up information that can only be obtained by insiders.

There are so many variables in making such a choice that we have probably touched only the surface. However, we feel that such a process of rationalization is necessary. You cannot afford to make many mistakes. You don't have the time.

Should you be totally uncommitted to a specific location — whether for business or personal reasons — then you might want to survey this vast and wonderful land from coast-to-coast and see what it has to offer.

Each year some book or magazine article reports a survey that selects the "best cities" for living, business, or both. Since lifestyle at any time, but especially at age 50 and up, becomes very germane to the relocation choice, the various factors we have advanced previously need to be considered. If a survey says Atlanta, Austin, Pittsburgh, San Diego, Seattle, Baltimore, or Tampa are the best cities, then you have to ask: By what criteria were these cities picked? Do these criteria meet my own? Or were they chosen for the "average" forty-year-old corporate employee with one wife and two school-age children? Certainly, circumstances alter cases.

Before we get down to the nitty-gritty, let's look at another factor: cost-of-living. If you are totally retired, if you are being transferred and the company is picking up the cost-of-living differential, or if you are opening a new business or buying one, your income will be grossly affected. As a retiree, your income is pretty well fixed, even if you get small cost-of-inflation increments. Major cost-of-living items, therefore, should be taken into account. For example:

San Diego is a wonderful town for living, but average electric bills were recently reported at $1,144 a year. In the city of Akron, they were less than $300. Income tax in Baltimore averaged $2,500, whereas in Tampa it was $0. A 3-bedroom home in average Smalltown, USA came to $85,000, while in San Diego, California or Cambridge, Massachusetts, it got up to $350,000. Crime in Washington, DC claims two or three lives every 24 hours, while Madison, Wisconsin was judged the safest city in all of America.

You see that variables will make a whale of a difference in your selection. But let some statistics speak for themselves and help you make your choices (cities mentioned include suburbs in their respective metropolitan areas):

## BEST PLACES TO START A BUSINESS

- Austin, TX
- Dallas, TX
- Huntsville, AL
- Orlando, FL
- El Paso, TX
- Atlanta, GA
- Nashville, TN
- San Antonio, TX
- Charleston, SC
- Tampa/St. Petersburg, FL

## BEST SURVIVAL CITIES FOR BUSINESS START-UPS

- Manchester/Nashua, NH
- Raleigh/Durham, NC
- Nashville, TN
- Boston, MA
- Washington, D.C.

- South Bend, IN/
  Benton Harbor, MI
- Atlanta, GA
- Fort Wayne, IN
- Orlando, FL
- Austin, TX

*(Note: Four cities show up on both of the above lists —
Atlanta, Austin, Nashville, and Orlando.)*

## FASTEST GROWING METROPOLITAN AREAS (PROJECTED TO 1995)

- Fort Myers, FL
- Naples, FL
- Fort Pierce, FL
- Anaheim/Santa Ana, CA
- W. Palm Beach/Boca Raton/Delray Beach, FL
- Ocala, FL
- Orlando, FL
- Santa Rosa/Petaluma, CA
- Bryan/College Station (near Austin), TX
- Fort Collins/Loveland, CO

## BEST PLACES FOR QUALITY OF LIFE

- Albuquerque, NM
- Birmingham, AL
- Charlotte, NC
- Columbus, OH
- Fort Worth, TX

- Orlando, FL
- Portland, OR
- Providence, RI
- Sacramento, CA
- St. Paul, MN

## FASTEST GROWING METROPOLITAN AREAS (1980 TO 1988)

| | |
|---|---|
| Naples, FL | 61.1% |
| Ocala, FL | 55.0 |
| Fort Pierce, FL | 53.3 |
| Fort Myers, FL | 50.6 (incl. Cape Coral) |
| Melbourne, FL | 42.3 (incl. Titusville) |
| W. Palm Beach, FL | 41.9 (incl. Boca Raton, Delray) |
| Austin, TX | 39.5 |
| Orlando, FL | 38.8 |
| Fort Walton Beach, FL | 37.0 |
| Las Cruces, NM | 37.0 |

## FASTEST GROWING METROPOLITAN AREAS

| (1988) | (1989) |
|---|---|
| Austin, TX | Manchester/Nashua, NH |
| Manchester/Nashua, NH | Orlando, FL |
| Orlando, FL | W. Palm Beach, FL |
| Phoenix, AZ | Raleigh/Durham, NC |
| Atlanta, GA | Washington, DC |
| Raleigh/Durham, NC | Las Vegas, NV |
| Huntsville, AL | Atlanta, GA |
| Washington, DC | Anaheim, CA |
| Dallas/Ft. Worth, TX | Portsmouth, NH |
| San Diego, CA | Phoenix, AZ |

## SLOWER-PACED CITIES
## WITH LOWEST INCIDENT OF HEART DISEASE

- Houston, TX
- San Jose, CA
- Oxnard, CA
- Atlanta, GA
- Dallas, TX

- Salt Lake City, UT
- Memphis, TN
- E. Lansing, MI
- Los Angeles, CA
- San Francisco, CA

## CITIES WITH HIGHEST INCIDENT
## OF HEART DISEASE

- New York, NY
- Buffalo, NJ
- Providence, RI
- Worcester, MA
- Columbus, OH*

- Youngstown, OH
- Springfield, MA
- Canton, OH
- Boston, MA

*(*overall pace only)*

## TOP-TEN FAST-GROWTH STATES
(New jobs, new companies, climate for growth)

| (1988) | (1989) | (1990) | |
|---|---|---|---|
| Arizona | Nevada | Nevada | 50.7%+ |
| New Hampshire | New Hampshire | Alaska | 37.4 |
| Maryland | Virginia | Arizona | 36.0 |
| Florida | Maryland | Florida | 33.4 |
| Virginia | Georgia | California | 26.1 |
| Georgia | Florida | N. Hampshire | 21.0 |
| Delaware | Delaware | Texas | 19.9 |
| Nevada | North Carolina | Georgia | 19.1 |
| California | Tennessee | Washington | 18.3 |
| Tennessee | California | Utah | 18.3 |

## FORTUNE'S TOP-TEN CITIES 1989
## AND COST-OF-LIVING INDEX*

| | |
|---|---|
| Dallas, TX | 94* |
| Atlanta, GA | 97 |
| Kansas City, MO | 95 |
| Los Angeles, CA | 138 |
| Baltimore, MD | 115 |
| New York, NY | 134 |
| San Francisco, CA | 133 (Bay Area) |
| Pittsburgh, PA | 99 |
| Portland, OR | 100 |
| Minneapolis/St. Paul, MN | 104 |

## INC.'S TOP-TEN CITIES 1990

- Las Vegas, NV
- Washington, DC
- Orlando, FL
- Tallahassee, FL
- San Jose, CA
- Atlanta, GA
- Charleston, SC
- Lincoln, NB
- Raleigh/Durham, NC
- Anaheim, CA

## FORTUNE'S TOP-TEN CITIES 1990 AND PRO-BUSINESS RANKING

| | |
|---|---|
| Atlanta, GA | #2 |
| Dallas/Ft. Worth, TX | 13 |
| Pittsburgh, PA | 8 |
| Kansas City, MO | 10 |
| Nashville, TN | 4 |
| Salt Lake City, UT | 13 (tie) |
| Charlotte, NC | 1 |
| Orlando, FL | 10 |
| Austin, TX | 13 (tie) |
| Phoenix, AZ | 21 |

*Also highly rated are West Palm Beach, Florida,*
*Seattle, Washington, and Louisville, Kentucky.*

## MONEY MAGAZINE TOP-TEN METROPOLITAN AREAS

| (1989) | (1990) |
|---|---|
| Seattle, WA | Bremerton, WA |
| Danbury, CT | Seattle, WA |
| San Francisco, CA | San Francisco, CA |
| Denver, CO | Tacoma, WA |
| Nashua, NJ | Columbia, MO |
| Boston, MA | Eugene/Springfield, OR |
| Boston North Shore, MA | Minneapolis/St. Paul, MN |
| Central New Jersey, NJ | Olympia, WA |
| Minneapolis/St. Paul, MN | Sacramento, CA |
| Pittsburgh, PA | Los Angeles, CA |

## 17 BEST AREAS FOR COMMERCIAL REAL ESTATE INVESTMENT, 1991

| | |
|---|---|
| Seattle, WA | 6.4 on scale of 10:1 |
| San Francisco, CA | 6.2 |
| Los Angeles, CA | 6.0 |
| Washington, DC | 5.6 |
| Chicago, IL | 5.6 |
| San Diego, CA | 5.4 |
| Dallas, TX | 5.4 |
| Houston, TX | 5.2 |
| Philadelphia, PA | 4.4 |
| Atlanta, GA | 4.4 |
| St. Louis, MO | 3.8 |
| New York, NY | 3.8 |
| Detroit, MI | 3.7 |
| Miami, FL | 3.7 |
| Boston, MA | 3.5 |
| Phoenix, AZ | 3.3 |
| Denver, CO | 3.1 |

## TOP-TEN MOVE DESTINATIONS (RYDER TRUCK RENTAL SURVEY 1990)

- Las Vegas, NV
- Milwaukee, WI
- Reno, NV
- Tulsa, OK
- Grand Rapids, MI
- Albuquerque, NM
- Corpus Christi, TX
- Harrisburg, PA
- Madison, WI
- Indianapolis, IN

## CARBON DIOXIDE POLLUTION 1988, WORST STATES

| | |
|---|---|
| Texas | 575 million metric tons |
| California | 312 |
| Pennsylvania | 256 |
| Ohio | 251 |

Other states with high emissions:

| | | |
|---|---|---|
| Florida | Georgia | Illinois |
| Indiana | Kentucky | Louisiana |
| Michigan | New York | Ohio |

## OFFICE MARKET SURVEY, 1990, ANNUAL RENTAL COST PER SQUARE FOOT

| | |
|---|---|
| Washington, DC | $49 |
| New York (Midtown) | $45 |
| Boston, MA | $41 |
| Chicago, IL | $39 |
| Los Angeles, CA | $35 |
| Hartford, CT | $34 |
| Phoenix, AZ | $29 |
| Minneapolis, MN | $29 |
| Atlanta, GA | $29 |
| San Francisco, CA | $28 |

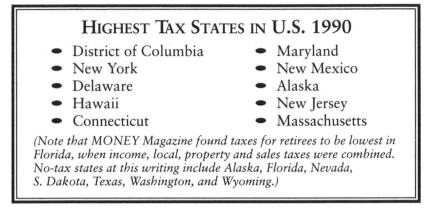

HIGHEST TAX STATES IN U.S. 1990

- District of Columbia
- New York
- Delaware
- Hawaii
- Connecticut

- Maryland
- New Mexico
- Alaska
- New Jersey
- Massachusetts

*(Note that MONEY Magazine found taxes for retirees to be lowest in Florida, when income, local, property and sales taxes were combined. No-tax states at this writing include Alaska, Florida, Nevada, S. Dakota, Texas, Washington, and Wyoming.)*

A comparison of this random selection of state and metropolitan area statistics will give you some idea and may be used as a guide. It is recommended, however, that later changes be checked out with local chambers of commerce or economic development agencies.

## RETIREMENT OPTIONS IN NEARBY FOREIGN LOCATIONS

It is unlikely that you will be planning to open a business or to seek new employment in a foreign country — unless a company places you out of the United States. However, among foreign countries that are acceptable risks are Canada, which is English-speaking (except for the Province of Quebec where a knowledge of French is almost mandatory), and Mexico, where a moderate ten percent inflation factor and a recent free trade agreement have created some attractive potentials.

At this time, in 1991, unsettled conditions in a number of countries make a move there unlikely. The U.S. State Department has marked the following high-risk areas: Peru, El Salvador, India, Turkey, Colombia, Philippines, Sri Lanka, Northern Ireland, Nicaragua, and possibly Spain. The entire Mid-East is to be treated with caution, except for Israel, unless you are of Arabic background.

The only Central-South American country that we would consider as a retirement-and-business location would be Costa

Rica. It has an established American colony and a benevolent attitude toward Yankee-run businesses. Favored are export businesses that are labor-intensive. A knowledge of Spanish is desirable, of course, and a thorough visit of the country, especially Costa Rica's benign capital of San Jose, is recommended. The American Chamber of Commerce and English newspaper, *Tico Times,* will be helpful.

The Caribbean Islands have been an attraction for vacationers, retirees, and businesspeople since George Washington was a young man. From the U.S. perspective, these islands might all look alike, but each has a personality of its own. With the demise of the British Empire and the virtual decline of other European authority, native administrations are largely in command. With the exceptions of the Cayman Islands, St. Bartholomew and a few very tiny ones, the islands are governed and run primarily by black populations. Puerto Rico and Dominican Republic (for the time being we will have to gloss over Cuba) are dominated by Hispanic people. In any event, doing business is the islands is fraught with some problems, even though the physical attractions are substantial and the local governments welcome Yankee dollars and ingenuity — especially if these can be translated into labor-intensive industries and exports.

Here is a brief survey of the major islands, all subject to change from year to year. Any U.S. retiree seriously interested in living and working or doing business here should, if he or she has not already done so, spend some time on the island or islands of choice. Talk to other business people, principally the commissioner of commerce and industry, about any of your concerns, such as licenses and taxes, labor supply, training, landing costs, etc.

*Antigua.* Formerly British. 171 sq. mi.; pop. 60,000; capital St. John's, 36,000. Tourism; cotton, sugar; livestock; rum, lobsters.

*Bahamas.* Formerly British. 700 islands on 5,400 sq. mi. 250,000; Nassau, 110,000; 85% Black. Tourism; fruits and vegetables.

*Barbados.* Formerly British. 166 sq. mi.; pop. 260,000; Bridgetown, 7,500. Tourism; rum; light mfg.; some crude oil and natural gas.

*British Virgin Islands.* 40 islands, 15 inhabited. 59 sq. mi.; pop.
13,000; 90% Black. Tourism; rum; boating; fishing.
*Cayman Islands.* British. 25,000 people on 100 sq. mi. (3
islands); 20% Black, 40% mixed. Tourism; banking, tax
haven.
*Dominican Republic.* Hispanic culture. With Haiti, 23rd
largest island; pop. 7 million. Tourism; sugar; ferro-nickel,
gold mining.
*French West Indies.* French. Guadeloupe (350,000 — 90%
Black/mulatto) and Martinique (same as Guadeloupe). 1,100
sq. mi.; capital Ford de France, 110,000; Export crops.
*Grenada.* 133 sq. mi.; 85,000 inh.; mainly Black. Capital St.
George's, 7,500. Cocoa beans, nutmeg, mace, bananas;
little tourism.
*Netherland Antilles.* Curacao (100,000), Bonaire, Aruba
(65,000; nom. indep.) Capital Willemstad. Tourism; petro
products; light manufacturing. New U.S. tax treaty with
Aruba.
*Puerto Rico.* Commonwealth under U.S. flag. Free trade zones
and tax incentives for plant locations in underdeveloped areas.
Over three million people; 650,000 in San Juan. Culture:
Hispanic/American. Tourism; light industry; fishing,
handicrafts; construction.
*U.S. Virgin Islands.* St. Thomas (busiest tourist hub in the
Caribbean), St. Croix (largest in land area) and St. John. U.S.
possession since 1917. 136 sq. mi.; pop. 110,000; major town
Charlotte Amalie (St. Thomas); 15,000. 80% Black. Tourism;
some refining; rum; charter boating. Tax advantages,
especially in St. Croix industrial parks.

For more information on Caribbean trade opportunities and
general information, contact:

Caribbean Tourism Association, 20 E. 46th St., New York, NY
10164
Eastern Caribbean Tourism Association, 220 E. 42 St.,
New York, NY 10017
Caribbean Basin Trade and Business Investment Center,
U.S. Department of Commerce, (202) 377-2527

Caribbean/Central American Action Group, 1333 New
Hampshire Ave., NW, Washington, DC 20036, (202) 466-7464

## IF YOU DO HAVE TO MOVE...

Contact a large moving company or association that might have
handy moving kits to make your job easier. Here is a chance,
too, to sell off what you really don't need. Remember that your
junk might be somebody else's treasure. And it will be such fun
to buy new things — which might be quite different, if you move
to a sub-tropical climate. So in case you do move, here is some
sound advice from the moving industry.

Moving companies provide a variety of services for a range
of fees. It is a good idea to talk with different movers to compare their services. To find out who the best movers are in your
area, begin by asking your friends about their experiences with
the movers they have used. You can also check with the Better
Business Bureau.

Once you have compiled a list of movers, inform them of the
destination and timing of your move. Ask them to explain their
estimates in detail and to give you a copy. Then carefully compare to see which mover best suits your needs and budget.

If you are moving interstate, you should read and understand all of the information you will receive. In addition to bro-
chures explaining their various services, moving companies should
give you a copy of the Interstate Commerce Commission's consumer advice booklet and the company's latest performance report.

It is important to try to make arrangements for your move
well in advance, preferably four to six weeks before the moving
date. You should also discuss with your mover the following
aspects of your move:

- Rates and charges.
- The mover's liability for your belongings.
- How pickup and delivery work.
- What claims protection you have.

## PACKING

Proper packing by a trained packer using specially designed cartons and materials is crucial to a good move. Schedule a packing
day for the mover, a day or two before the moving van is loaded.

Be present when your goods are packed, or arrange for someone to be there. Before packing, an inventory will be made of
your household goods being shipped. Make sure all copies of the
inventory are legible and that all items are numbered, listed and
described correctly. Have valuable items listed separately on the
inventory. Discuss the inventory sheet with your mover and make
sure you agree with the list of your possessions before you sign it.

The inventory record is one of your most important shipping documents. You will need to refer to it at your destination
and will be asked to sign it again after you have received and in-
spected your goods.

## PLANNING YOUR MOVING DAY

Your mover may ask you to select several consecutive days during which your goods can be loaded and a second series of dates
during which your goods can be delivered to your new home. A
spread of days gives you and your mover the flexibility needed
to keep your move on schedule. If you desire pickup on a special
date, ask your mover about the conditions of this arrangement.

There may be an unforeseeable delay in pickup. It is best not
to plan to relinquish your house until several days after the period
in which your goods were to have been picked up.

## MOVING DAY

- Be on hand when the movers arrive to answer questions and
  give directions.
- Discuss the delivery arrangements fully with your mover.
- Have beds stripped and ready to be packed.
- Save your energy by letting the moving crew take beds apart,
  roll up carpets, and put mattresses in cartons.
- Read the Bill of Lading (the contract between you and the
  mover) before you sign it. Keep it with you until your

shipment is delivered, all charges are paid, and all claims, if any, are settled.

- Tell your mover where you or your representative can be reached at your destination.

- While shipment is in transit, keep in contact with the mover's agent at your destination.

## MONEY MATTERS

The cost of interstate moves is usually based on the weight of your belongings and on the distance they are shipped, plus packing and other services. Some movers are basing costs on the amount of space your belongings occupy in the moving van (volume) instead of on their weight. All rates that movers charge have been approved by the Interstate Commerce Commission.

*Weighing Your Shipment.* Before the van driver loads your shipment, he weighs the van on a certified scale. After your shipment is loaded, he weighs the van a second time. The difference between the two weights is the net weight of your shipment, upon which final charges are based.

*Liability of the Moving Company.* Your mover will explain his liability under federal regulations for any loss of or damage to your property. In addition to the company's basic liability, there are other options available for increasing the amount of coverage you can place on your possessions, which your mover will be glad to explain. We recommend you consider this extra coverage to protect the full value of your shipment.

*Payment on Delivery.* Before your household goods are delivered and unloaded, be ready to pay the van driver in cash, money order, traveler's check or cashier's check as specified by the carrier beforehand, unless other arrangements have been made with the moving company, in accordance with state or federal laws. The driver is not allowed to provide change.

On an interstate shipment, if the billed charges are more than the non-binding, written estimate, you are liable for the estimate, plus ten percent of the balance at the time of the delivery. Any amount remaining to be paid is due in thirty days.

# PLANNING

*Failure to plan for retirement means planning for failure. If you do something about it — even if you do a little bit of planning — you'll have a smoother transition. And there'll be more options open to you...Retirement is a time when you can realize your dream. Retirement won't go away. You'll be there.*

—Elsie K. Perlmutter

Retirement Planner

# CHAPTER IX

### SPRINGBOARD TO SATISFACTION AND $$$

Paul K. volunteered to counsel members of the local AARP organization as well as foreign entrepreneurs in two Latin American countries for the International Executive Service Corps (I.E.S.C.). One day he received a call from a counseling-for-profit company, which ultimately hired him to be their representative for real paychecks.

Esther P. was a retired teacher in the public school system. As a volunteer, she taught new immigrants at a weekly English for Speakers of Other Languages (ESOL) class, helping them learn English and become Americans. When opportunities arose to do substitute ESOL teaching at a local high school, she was tagged for the part-time job at net rates of about $75 a day.

David B., having retired from the export business, took on the volunteer job of international trade expert with SCORE, an agency subsidized by the U.S. Small Business Administration. Less than two years later, the executive director of the organization departed, and David was offered the job — at $50,000 a year.

Gustav B., this writer, also volunteered to become communications director for SCORE. The additional experience, reputation, and contacts enabled me to write a series of ten small business books — this book is one. A new career was launched from the springboard of volunteerism.

Volunteerism, when taken seriously, is a very satisfying but demanding job. Its remuneration is primarily the satisfaction of

175

giving back some of the good that society has bestowed upon us. Occasionally, in the process of rendering *pro bono* or gratuitous service to others, we come across an opportunity to turn our free help into paid activity.

This chapter is concerned with various aspects of satisfying volunteerism that are available to us. Sometimes these contacts and experts can be converted into new careers, quite different from those we might have pursued during our working life. The opportunities are quite endless; the needs forever. What we do with them is up to us.

The country's leading volunteer membership organization is probably the American Association of Retired People. With well over 25 million members, it offers dozens of programs through its national headquarters in Washington, DC or Long Beach, California, and the hundreds of chapters across the country.

Among programs that invite seniors to participate are: health advocacy, criminal justice, tax help, social outreach, widowed persons service, divorce crises, mature driving aid, legal counsel for elderly, retirement planning, worker equity, minority affairs, consumer affairs, housing information, senior environmental problems, job re-entry workshops, and publications such as AARP Bulletins, pertinent books, and *Modern Maturity* magazine.

Robert B. Maxwell, president of AARP, said that "volunteerism has always been a basic ingredient of our democratic form of government. From Colonial days to the present, our nation has been built through the efforts of volunteers working together to achieve a common goal."

He noted that already in 1830, when the French political philosopher/historian Alexis de Tocqueville visited America, he was amazed at the extent of citizen participation he found here. "The health of a democratic society," he said at the time, "may be measured by the quality of functions performed by private citizens."

Among the notable volunteer activities available to retirees are the following:

Senior Legislature of California, c/o Commission on Aging, Sacramento, CA. The mock legislature meets every Fall in California's state capital to draft legislation affecting the state's four million senior citizens. An eleven-year member is 71-year-old Gladys Hotchkiss of San Bernardino who also heads a fortnightly cable-TV forum on senior legislation.

Senior Environmental Employment Program (SEE) is sponsored by the Environmental Protection Agency throughout the U.S. It recruits retired chemists, engineers, technicians, researchers, analysts, and even wildlife experts. Most of the 1200 recruits work on local groundwater contamination problems, but one man in Idaho tracks mountain lions for tagging with radio collars. "Volunteers" even get paid — $6 to $15 an hour, paid by a $51 million EPA grant.

The U.S. Peace Corps Volunteer Recruitment Service is branching out to include more and more seniors and is becoming more entrepreneurial minded, too. Its more than 125,000 volunteers are in Hungary teaching English, on the Pacific island of Tuvalu planning an energy plant, in Honduras helping small farmers, in Morocco helping the sheep industry, in Niger controlling health problems. One is a nursing instructor in Gambia, a doctor in Papua, or a teacher trainer in the Philippines. Overseas assignments are for one or two years and carry a moderate expense stipend, as well as a re-adjustment bonus upon return. The Peace Corps can be contacted on the ninth floor at 1990 K St., NW, Washington, DC 20526, or phone toll free, 1-800-424-8580, extension 93.

SCORE is the Service Corps of Retired Executives. Headquartered in Washington, DC in a wing of the Small Business Administration, it has 385 field offices, usually in federal buildings, post office buildings, chambers of commerce, and community colleges. SCORE has over 12,000 men and women members who counsel, free and confidentially, hundreds of thousands of entrepreneurs and others who are exploring starting a business. They hold low-cost workshops in at least half of the locations. Their nearest location may be found in the blue section of your telephone directory under "SBA".

Besides local hospitals, churches, synagogues, libraries, and charitable organizations like the Red Cross, Salvation Army, American Cancer Society, and the various ones concerned with specific health problems, your city or county might have a volunteer corps or could be persuaded to organize one.

In Montgomery County, just north of Washington, DC, the county government formed Volunteer Opportunities for Retired

Professionals. It was founded in 1983 by two retired government employees and focuses on technical and managerial assistance to governmental and non-profit entities. Among volunteer assignments are claims review for the county attorney, reviews of various county control agencies in order to economize their operations, emergency management and civil defense work, consumer affairs counsels, and development of software for individual county departments.

Of the numerous environmental volunteer organizations that have developed in the past decade, one of interest is Earthwatch. It is similar to the Peace Corps, but organizes expeditions to research sites all over the world. Staff volunteers assist scholars and scientists in projects ranging from archaeological digs to cultural liaisons in China, to preserving endangered species and installation of conservation programs in the Aleutians or Amazonia. Earthwatch is twenty years old and located at 680 Mt. Auburn St., Watertown, MA 02272.

To show what becomes of our "retired" peers when they get tired of being retired, we will throw the spotlight on a handful of intrepid volunteers whose actions belie their ages.

Rosemary Park, 84, is a retired educator with a Ph.D. She formed the Plato Society (Perpetual Learning and Teaching Organization), a discussion group of about 400 members, divided into groups of fifteen. Members are all of professional background and average 65 years in age. Plato operates out of UCLA in Los Angeles.

Grant Cushinberry is a local Santa with a twenty-year record for organizing Thanksgiving dinners among Topeka, Kansas, poor families. In 1990, eight thousand were served. He also has arranged to rent out an entire movie house and invite one thousand underprivileged children to a free show, or to a visiting circus performance. When not busy with such activities, he collects clothing and household goods from the town, displays them on his "God's Little Half Acre" property and tells poor folks to come and help themselves.

Morris Kalmus is a volunteer with JACS, the Joint Action in Community Service of Philadelphia, PA. He's been counseling and helping young men returning from stints in the Job Corps. His forte is to get them back into school to finish their education, or to find them jobs. More than 500 young men have benefited from his ten years of devotion to the needs of an underclass.

Helping rural women better their standards of living is the aim of Associated Country Women of the World. A leader in the USA branch is Fayola Muchow, who has been all over rural America and in many foreign countries for the past thirty years, as good will ambassador. She also works with the 4-H and National Extension Homemakers Council, in addition to helping her husband run a 200-hog farm near Sioux Falls, South Dakota.

Lena Meekins is a Trenton Central High School security guard. Here she has an opportunity to recruit girls from nine to seventeen who need guidance and discipline. For the past twenty years, she has organized them into the New Breed Drill Team where Meekins tries to instill in her girls qualities of leadership, loyalty, and staying power. This structured activity has launched many young girls into life, better equipped to cope with its vagaries. Last year, a large group of alumni gave Mrs. Meekins a huge thank-you dinner.

Len Farr is a third-generation hardware store owner in Coos Bay, Oregon, and a staunch member of SCORE and the Rotary Club. For the latter organization he, often accompanied by his wife, has travelled many times to underdeveloped countries where Rotary International has undertaken supportive programs. As an example, he had local villagers in Guatemala install a pure water system and got Rotary to support it with a contribution of more than $6000 — a check for which he delivered in person when the project was completed.

For more than a decade, Jen Southworth of Bremerton, WA has been tutoring students in English writing, speaking, and reading. She has also trained more than 300 other volunteers become tutors, thus spreading literacy like a pebble tossed into a pond which makes concentric circles. Among her pupils was a semi-literate businessman, a high school dropout. As a result of Miss Southworth's efforts, he became highly successful and quadrupled his income. "To see their faces when they really understand," she said of her charges, "is really heaven on earth."

Adult education is spreading around the country like wildfire. Elderhostel programs have proliferated around the world for men and women who can afford the $250 to $3500 sessions. CUNY in New York City counts more than 6,000 students who are over 65. And in downtown New York, NYU's School of Continuing Education has become one the world's largest schools for the elderly. Harvard has a fifteen-year-old program entitled Institute for Learning in Retirement, attracting professionals between fifty and ninety years of age. Rather than failing in learning capacity, a Penn State study by Schaie-Willis found that "students" between sixty-four and ninety-five actually increased their mental functions once they started learning again.

Eckerd College in sunny St. Petersburg, Florida, has taken elderly education a step further. The school opened a 140-person condominium on the urban campus where volunteers can live. Most of them have become members of the college's Academy of Senior Professionals and act as part-time instructors as well as take classes and give guidance to younger undergraduates.

Creative retirement has become a way of life among 16,000 of Asheville's (NC) 62,000 residents. One thousand five hundred have signed up for participation in that city's Center for Creative Retirement. In the center's non-credit College for Seniors, retirees can further their education, pass on their knowledge to younger generations as volunteers, and become leaders in local hospitals and penal institutions. This interactive volunteer group has become one of President Bush's 1000 Points of Light. Information can be obtained from the CCR by sending a self-addressed, stamped envelope to them at UNC, Asheville, NC 28804-3299.

Like reading, research and visits to libraries? So does 75-year-young Dorothy Greenwald. She has been giving library tours to visitors for years as a volunteer of the New York Public Library. As an outgrowth, she is hired regularly by psychologists, architects, and other professionals to do research for them at the library's 42nd Street Reading Room. Her husband is a volunteer counselor with the Manhattan SCORE office. However, his expertise in construction know-how has come to the attention of the Federal Emergency Management Agency, which has hired him on several occasions for paid assistance, for as much as $1,000 a week.

To establish a working volunteer program is as complicated as starting a new company. In fact, organizing and managing volunteer organizations is in itself a distinct and highly profitable profession. In the Washington, DC area are probably in excess of two thousand associations, many of them non-profits, that are in most cases professionally managed by experts in management, fund-raising, public relations, and membership recruiting.

The following is a thirteen-point plan for the setting up of a professional volunteer program. Another excellent resource is to study a number of back-issues of *Association Management* magazine.

## ELEMENTS OF A SUCCESSFUL VOLUNTEER PROGRAM

1. **PLANNING**

   Planning is the key to success in all administrative responsibilities, and volunteer management is no exception. But planning for volunteers includes several unique actions, including the need to determine:

   - exactly *why* volunteers are wanted;
   - exactly *what* volunteers are expected to do;
   - what *resources* will be necessary to support volunteers, including requirements for space, equipment, furniture and supplies;
   - *who* will provide training and ongoing supervision of volunteers — and what preparation these key people will need;
   - *how many hours* of work it will take to accomplish the task (not how many people).

2. **VOLUNTEER JOB DESCRIPTIONS**

   If an assignment cannot be described in writing, it probably isn't a job. To assure effective utilization of volunteers, it is necessary to define the work to be done with as many specifics as possible. Volunteer job descriptions should, at a minimum, define: a title for the position; the purpose/rationale of the assignment; the scope of the work to be done (giving both the potentials and limits of the job); training and supervision plan; and time frames necessary.

3. **RECRUITMENT/PUBLIC RELATIONS**

   "Public relations" is what is necessary to make an organization visible to the public. If people do not know what a program is or does, they are hardly likely to volunteer to join it. "Recruitment" is the process of encouraging people to give their time and energy to the organization. The best recruitment is targeted to the audiences most likely to have the skills and interests to match the available volunteer job descriptions.

4. **SCREENING AND SELECTION**
   Many supervision and management problems can be prevented by effective initial interviewing of prospective volunteers. Also, the process of matching a new volunteer with the most appropriate assignment is key to assure ongoing motivation. The screening and selection period is the time to discuss expectations on both sides and to begin to set standards.

5. **ORIENTATION**
   Orientation is the overview of the total organization necessary for every volunteer, regardless of specific assignment. It places the work into context and allows for consistent introduction of policies, procedures, rights, and responsibilities.

6. **TRAINING**
   Training is individualized and should vary with the demands of each specific job description and the background each volunteer brings to the organization. There is the need for initial start-up training, plus the need for ongoing, in-service training. Much "training" is really the giving of good instructions, and often is integrated into the overall supervision plan.

7. **SUPERVISION**
   As with salaried staff, volunteer staff need support from those in a position to see the total picture and who know what work needs to be done. For volunteers, however, a key aspect of supervision is access to someone in charge during the time the volunteer is on duty.

8. **RECOGNITION**
   Recognition is one way to "pay" volunteers for their efforts, but it has many nuances. If there are annual dinners and certificates, but no daily support, recogni-

tion can speak with "forked tongue." While formalized
thank you events are important, informal recognition is
more important. This includes everything from simple
courtesy to including volunteers in staff meetings and
decision-making. It is also part of recognition to offer
constructive criticism, since such training implies a
belief that the volunteer can do even better work.

9. **COORDINATION**
   By definition, volunteers are part-time staff. A volunteer
   program can have people who work schedules ranging
   from one afternoon a week to four days a week; morn-
   ings and evenings; alternate Sundays; February off to go
   to Florida; July off to go camping — etc.! Add to this
   the diversity of the people who volunteer (all ages, backgrounds, physical conditions) and you end up with an
   amazing logistical challenge. A volunteer program must
   have a *leader* and that leader must be able to coordinate
   all the details of scheduling and assigning.

10. **RECORDKEEPING AND REPORTING**
    If volunteers are important to the work of an organiza-
    tion, then it is important to know what volunteers are
    doing. Such documentation assists in recruitment, train-
    ing, recognition, and fundraising (volunteer hours can be
    applied to in-kind match). For purposes of insurance and
    to back up the income tax deduction claims of volun-
    teers, recordkeeping is also necessary. Once records are
    kept, they are of little meaning if they are not reported.
    Reports of cumulative achievements of volunteers should
    be shared routinely with volunteers themselves, as well
    as with administration or funding sources.

11. **EVALUATION**
    It is a sin to waste the time of a volunteer. Therefore it
    is imperative that volunteer programs regularly evalu-
    atethe impact of services performed and whether those
    ser-vices are still necessary. Along with program evalua-
    tion, it is helpful to conduct individual performance
    review with volunteers, so as to maintain motivation
    and allow for personal growth.

12. **VOLUNTEER/SALARIED STAFF RELATIONS**
The interrelationship of volunteers and paid staff is the single biggest danger area, unless steps are taken early to encourage teamwork. There are numerous reasons why salaried staff is threatened by volunteers and also why volunteers are sometimes resistant to working with paid staff. This is a human relations issue with no easy answers, but it should be remembered that almost no professional/academic training program prepares salaried staff to work with volunteers. So some staff development on this topic is critical. It is also helpful to encourage paid staff to discuss their own, personal volunteer work outside of the organization to break down the barriers of "us" and "them."

13. **VOLUNTEER INPUT**
Too many organizations want help instead of input. Volunteers are in a position to observe the organization. They bring their hearts and hands, but also their brains and mouths. One benefit of having volunteers is that they can take more risks in criticizing or speaking out (they can also be effective advocates when they see things going well). But there must be a channel for this input or volunteers will either cause friction or leave. Also, having a clear way for volunteers to voice opinions develops their ownership of the volunteer program.

A *good*

*business manager*

*hires optimists as his*

*sales representatives*

*and pessimists to run*

*his credit department.*

# CHAPTER X

## OPPORTUNITIES IN THE CRYSTAL BALL
## IF YOU'RE ONLY IN YOUR FIFTIES...

If you are in this category, a score of years lies ahead of you in which you might want to start a business of your own or buy a business. Your options are plentiful, not only in your home town, but across the nation, and even in some friendly havens abroad.

Looking randomly at trends and opportunities, here are some types of businesses that stand out from the crowd and that promise to continue profitably within and beyond this decade. (Re-read chapter VIII, as well, in which we discuss choices and options for those who seek to relocate with the U.S.A. or abroad.)

*Environment:* The pollution of our globe breeds endless problems, but also offers many solutions and opportunities to the alert yet conscientious entrepreneur. There are twelve areas that concern themselves with the environment. All of them are, and will continue to be, magnets that can attract entrepreneurs. They include:

- Water resource management

- Forestry (88% of forestry management is in the hands of governments)

- Dam safety (46 states have laws governing dam construction and operation)

- Coastal zone management (50% is under federal control)

- Hazardous waste dumps

- Underground storage tanks, leakages, and replacements

- Indoor air pollution

- Other air pollution control facilities, such as industrial and commercial chimneys, automotive exhaust, et al.

- Groundwater protection

- Toxic air emission

- Property evaluation, testing, and remedial work to conform with environmental laws

- Permitting process, which includes inspection, testing, and required remedies for air emission, water discharges, solid and hazardous waste disposal

Specifically pin-pointing businesses that are growing and will blossom in the next decade and beyond, we can turn to a current book entitled *The Green Entrepreneur** which describes in some detail a number of environmental, entrepreneurial opportunities. (*McGraw-Hill 1991, $14.95 pb)

*Advertising:* Social marketing that extols moderation, conservation, healthier attitudes toward consumption. Many large corporations have begun recycling programs, often at considerable profits to themselves, have instituted conservation training among employees, and have discovered that environmentally-conscious promotion is simply good public relations — and good business.

*Agriculture:* Despite the apparent shrinkage of agricultural populations, we must eat and feed our growing numbers. The U.S. now is home to a quarter billion people. Society is not yet convinced that population pollution is the real problem. So we go on — trying to reduce reliance on pesticides and fertilizers, controlling the insatiable demand for irrigation through more efficient technology, and increasing crop yield per acre by more scientific production. In addition, we hanker for more *natural* foods, more elite crops, high-profit herbs, exotic fruits, leaner meats. Opportunities in agriculture are growing up all over the place, and more and more entrepreneurs are seeing in them rea-

sons for moving out of the congested cities and onto their own
*"God's Little Acre."* Taking inspiration from the World War II
victory gardens, one enterprising company in Massachusetts has
*leased* more than 5,000 fruit trees to city slickers, shipping their
trees' production to them in return for a rental fee of about $39.

Biotechnology is seeking high-yield, disease resistant crops as
well as synthetic pesticides that do not pollute the environment.
A Southern California company processes wet sludge and wood
wastes into recycled topsoil that is lauded by the EPA and the
Sierra Club. In Missouri and Virginia growers have developed
high-yield, profitable herb plantations that make costly near-
urban acres worth saving for agricultural exploitation.

Another Virginia farm generates humus by composting wood
stumps and landfill wastes, turning nearly 200,000 tons of debris
into usable soil enrichers. Even giant companies, such as Anheuser-
Busch, use formerly wasted beer sludge and reprocess it into nutri-
ent liquid sold for fertilizers, at the rate of fifty tons a day.

*Aquaculture:* Indoor and outdoor fish hatcheries are growing, and will continue to grow, as fishing in oceans becomes
more difficult and costly, while demand for "healthy" fish keeps
increasing. About a billion pounds of fish are raised annually in
more than 500 fisheries. It takes about $175,000 to install a
commercial hatchery, providing you have the land or buildings
to accommodate such an operation. The U.S. Department of
Agriculture, comparable state departments, and universities with
agricultural departments (such as Lehigh University, Bethlehem,
Pennsylvania) are doing much research in aquaculture and can
assist entrepreneurs in launching a business.

*Automotive Industry:* Solar-energy propelled and electrically-
operated vehicles will grow in popularity and utility as technology
improves and makes such alternate fuel use economically feasible.
It goes without saying that the benefits of reducing aerial pollution from burning fossil fuels in cars is of immeasurable benefit
to all of mankind. However, the business opportunities in these
trends are even more limitless.

Repair shops that operate "environmentally" are making
themselves heard. They recycle polluting oils and wastes; assure
that no Freon, asbestos, and anti-freeze is poured into sewers
and dumps; and dispose of old batteries in a safe manner.

The more than 130,000 gas stations in the U.S., especially the older ones, present disquieting problems to the environment. Old underground tanks can spring leaks and pollute underground water supplies. The EPA and state agencies everywhere have pounced on this problem with stringent laws and regulations. This *discovery* has, in turn, opened up opportunities in underground testing, repair, and replacement of tanks— the latter at costs averaging $40,000. The latter, collaterally, also opens opportunities in engineering, soil testing, financing, and insurance.

*Beauty products:* Milady's face and body, despite attempts at "equalization" of the sexes, will continue to require lotions and potions — but with a possible difference. There is a discernible trend toward more *natural* products, and a definite bridging of the consumer, as more men, too, use cosmetics and exotic lotions.

Proof of the success of *natural* cosmetic products is a British company started in 1976 that now does more than $150 million in business, including a considerable amount in the U.S. Smaller American companies like Tom's of Maine and Aveda Hair Products also use the new, ecologically-attuned approach to marketing and with considerable success.

*Biodegrading:* While this is hardly a single business, it is a concept that has caught on in America and even in the world consumer mind. Our landfills are becoming clogged and overflowing. In America, as in Europe, this problem is recognized as serious. At the same time, convenience goods, usually wrapped in plastics, are more and more in demand.

However, now comes a change. People are becoming conscious of the fact that diapers, coffee filters (white ones), and papers are not disappearing in underground dumps as had been supposed. Some tests of dumps that have been used for a couple of decades have shown that even newspapers can still be read twenty years after being buried in landfills. Next step: ultrasponge materials that decompose within 48 hours; biocompatible polymers; unbleached papers — all products of the present that will grow and develop in the future.

*Consulting:* This broad category is a natural for retirees who want to continue working productively. It will increase in future years as our world becomes more specialized, and as companies discover that even $50 to $150 an hour specialists are cost-effective when measured against salaried employees into whose income a 25% to 30% fringe cost factor must be added — not counting vacation, sickness, and unproductive coffee-break time.

Among consultants who are and will be needed and who can profit as *second careerists* are those familiar with:

- electronic data interchange — teaching a small business to become computer-efficient

- energy-efficiency experts for home and business, even entire municipalities

- production process efficiency experts, including time studies, water and fuel conservation, mechanical improvements

- government relations, including selling to governments, and avoiding possible complications with supervisory agencies such as EPA, FCC, FDA, IRS, OSHA, and those concerned with discrimination against minorities and women

- heating and cooling specialists

- office management in the decade of the environment — including recycling, biodegradability, pool transportation, leasing experts, community relations, traffic control, and even child care and preventative health care

- specialized activities that are used only occasionally, such as market research, publication development, employee and management training, internal and external security

(See also entry: "Becoming a Consultant").

*Day Care:* Since biology has a way of confounding population growth restrictions, we must take into account that in the present decade and in years to come, day care centers must proliferate. Such facilities have grown by leaps and bounds and are now recognized by businesses and industry as important and productive incentives. As more and more women enter the labor market, and since the production of babies continues apace, facilities for child day care need to be expanded. Often, corporations sponsor such facilities or enter into joint ventures with professional operators. They make such centers available to their employees either free or at subsidized rates, or even subsidize child care at private centers.

Babies are not the only ones who demand day care. Elderly parents or handicapped family members also demand day care in convenient and professionally operated facilities. Here are opportunities for retirees with instructional or health care backgrounds that are sure to go on and on, and grow with the years.

*Employment agencies:* A discernible trend during the past decade that promises to continue strongly into the rest of the century is the employment of temporary specialists, and more particular to our interests, of older men and women. Companies both large and small, well-established and start-ups, often find that seasonal demands make employment of short-term personnel advantageous. Part-timers and short-term employees are usually not subject to increasing pressures from unions and government strictures, nor need they be part of the benefit pool that can add as much as 30% to the cost of permanent employees.

Employment agencies have been formed that act *in loco parentis* to the employees they "lease" out to companies, like mobile equipment. Others, such as Retiree Skills, Inc. of Phoenix (see case histories in this book), focus on the fifty-and-up temps — offering silver-topped experience in place of youthful enthusiasm. Another trend that will continue strong is in the environmental field. A look at the big city employment pages reveals more and more help wanted ads under the rubric *Environmental*. Employment agenting in temps, elderly, and environmental specialists is indeed a g-r-o-w-i-n-g field and is relatively low in labor and financing demands.

*Fast Food Operations:* This hyperactive type of business might not be the stuff retirement careers are made of, but many an elderly parent becomes a partner, at least *pro tem,* with his offspring. Fast food businesses are big business and are likely to continue to be, as these eateries adapt themselves to modern nutritional demands. Trends include changes to healthier foods, to more buffet-style serving, biodegradable utensils, limitations on automatic water dispensing. Among desserts, frozen yogurts and other low-cholesterol "ice creams" are growing in demand, too, and are taking up the slack in any drop in richer ice cream sales. One good thing about this kind of business — when the operation gets slow, you can always eat the inventory.

Home delivery is not exactly a fast-food category, but it should be mentioned here, too. Shopping by phone will also be an increasingly important way of food merchandising, especially in metropolitan areas, among elderly, and with gourmet-style food stores. In areas inhabited by large numbers of elderly retirees, commercial meals-on-wheels restaurants are growing in utility and popularity. What is especially attractive in this business is that most transactions are done by "subscription" — that is, the customer arranges for regular daily or alternate-daily delivery of prepared foods. Another home-delivery business is that of the contractor, who arranges with several area restaurants, produces one combination menu, and arranges with area residents to deliver hot meals in a large variety of recipes — all at a slight mark-up, collecting a percentage from both supplier and ultimate customer.

*Green Thumb Enterprises:* Our environmental decade is spurring the growth of green things — trees, landscaping, flowers, herb gardens, vegetables. If you have been in this business or like the idea of green-thumbing, here is a business that will continue to be strong and even pleasurabe. In the southern climes of South Florida, South Texas, and Southern California, exotic fruits can be raised, or even much under-rated exotic berry-bushes like jojoba. All of these are high-value products. Interior plantscaping continues strong and architects and builders, domestically and in Europe, keep demands for fancy plants going. In many sections of the U.S. where such plants thrive, marketing is done most effectively through associations and co-operatives. Flower bouquet subscription services are another idea that can sprout profits year-around, and don't necessarily demand a large investment or facility. And don't forget eclectic gardening supplies. It's real *green* business.

*Inspirational Enterprises:* Religion and matters of the spirit are growing opportunities for imaginative, and inspired, marketers. Take religious bookstores. They focus on "clean" literature of Christian, Jewish or other persuasions. This category of literature, tapes, videos, and related merchandise has less obsolescence and usually sells at better-than-average mark-ups. It lends itself well to targeted mail order business. Having been around as long as man has been on this earth, religion, or inspirational enterprises, promise to have few recessions in the future. Just look at what is happening in the late, great Russian "hell"!

*High-Technology:* It would be spurious to anticipate all the opportunities around the corner that involve the wonders of tomorrow. But they are legion. Take, for example, the Workshop of Tomorrow — a roboticized laboratory developed and run by the U.S. Bureau of Standards and Technology in Gaithersburg, Maryland. Here Uncle Sam spends millions of dollars to develop avant-garde tools and processes that can be borrowed or bought by private entrepreneurs.

The field of computers changes every year and continues to be wide open for embellishments, innovations in both hardware and software, business or technology, graphics and medicine. Materials and material-handling come up with astounding new ways and means even before the ink is dry on the last promotion brochure. Transportation is facing revolutionary changes — such as automobiles running on solar power, or newly-efficient batteries that can propel a car for a full day, silently and without pollution at fifty or sixty miles per hour. Energy production and consumption will, and must, undergo radical changes in the coming decades if we are to survive as a nation, despite the obfuscation of the gasoline-nurtured automotive industry. Nutrition and medicine will go through unimagined changes, as we are faced, literally, with do-or-die decisions to maintain life for as long as we can. The pollution of our environment dictates that we are half-past-midnight in coming up with ecological solutions to our garbage problem and our mad dashes toward product-obsolescence.

Take just one specific opportunity in hi-tech: silica aerogels.

Next to some sponges and nature's masterpiece, the spider web, silica aerogels are the lightest man-made solids known at this time. NASA developed this product and it is becoming available to entrepreneurial applicators. A cube containing about twenty square feet weighs a pound (this is around the size of a household refrigerator!), yet it can support a ton of weight. The solid's application is in packaging, insulation, coatings, and who knows what else. For technical readers: silica aerogel is made of alcohol and silicon dioxide linked with a polymer. The mixture is heated under pressure and designed to be as light, as thick, and as sturdy as is required. At the present time, only the Department of Energy's Lawrence Livermore Laboratory in California produces it. Naturally it is impractical, even though it is twice as efficient as styrofoam — but the $4,000 price tag for a slab the size referred to above will some day come down to a cost-efficient number and be utilized in everything from picnic coolers to surfboards to skylights to satellites.

*Women in Business:* Two trends are discernible—more women continue to enter the marketplace, especially older women; and more women are going into businesses and *staying* in business. The statistics are awesome: while four out of five business people give up or go bankrupt during the first five years, the record of women-in-business is just the opposite — four out of five are still in business five years down the road. Are they more cautious? More persistent? Are their needs less? Even among the big women-owned businesses, successes are evident. Mary Kay and Avon Cosmetics are just two examples. Tupperware and Discovery Toys are two others — all heavily involving women in management and on the sales firing line, and all very successful. Among the fifteen million home based businesses, a majority are run by women. Even in the technology field, more and more women entrepreneurs can be seen — such as ASK Computer Systems, an $80 million software organization. A British import is Anita Roddick's fabulously successful Body Shops, with stores all across America. Jazzercize and numerous weight control centers are headed by women. All of them will proliferate and grow in market-share and income. An important factor for women entrepreneurs, now and even more in the future, is the technique of networking. There has not always been a great deal of support among women, but this situation is changing. Women are learning to work within organizations, especially on the more sophisticated executive level. Judith Mueller, Betty Phillips and Mary Jones developed I-CAN, a membership networking program, in the Washington, DC, area, to provide contacts for members. Retired women going back into the marketplace or exploring a business of their own can take heart from these trends and opportunities. I-CAN, the Information & Career Advisory Network, has put more than 3,000 women together with business opportunities at a fee income of more than $100,000. You might want to start such a network in your area.

## ENTREPRENEURIAL OPPORTUNITIES
## FOR THE UNDECIDED

A surprising number of men and women, having once retired and now contemplating return as re-born entrepreneurs, want to get into a business about which they know very little. This is not always so tragic. If the retiree has reached a reasonably ripe age, and accumulated a fair nest egg of extra cash, this new adventure into business is a just reward for a lifetime of hard work and thrift. Still — before spending the first $100, it would be well and wise to talk to others who have gone through similar revival stages, and to study up on the business of one's choice. Trade and professional journals are good sources to start with. *INC.*, *Success*, and *Entrepreneur* magazines offer monthly ideas to light the way. The latter publishes hundreds of business guides in hard copy and software, and, in some cases, on videos for $59.50 each for the printed guides. The complete catalog may be obtained by calling 1-800-421-2300. Some of the selections of special interest to newly un-retired "second careerists" include the following (Average net profit before taxes and average start-up investment is stated in the two figures following each entry. The return-on-investment ratio varies widely from 1:3 to 6:1. It often depends on what you *like* to be doing!):

Gift Baskets ($41,000 / $39,000) A great home business.
Information Broker ($60,000 / $20,000) For computer
    literate people.
Import/Export ($120,000 / $20,000) For experts only.
Wedding Planning Service ($60,000 / $13,000)
Mail Order Selling ($33,000+ / $23,000) A tricky business.
Seminars ($25,000+ / $25,000 - ) For specialists only.
Personal Shopping/Secretarial Services ($28,000 / $10,000)
Home Computer Services ($28,000 / $15,000)
    Newsletters, graphics.

Advertising Specialties ($30,000+ / $12,000) Salesmanship
& imagination.
Apartment Preparation Service ($35,000 / $16,000)
For handy Andies.
Collection Agency ($50,000 / $15,000) Credit or legal
background.
Consulting ($50,000+ / $5,000-$25,000) Be a specialist.
Recycling Consultant ($10,000-$50,000 / $50,000-
$150,000)
Temporary Help Agency ($25,000+ / $45,000+) Need 30-60
days capital.
Nanny/Day Care Helpers ($20,000+ / $60,000+)
Consignment/Resale Shop ($20,000 / $30,000+)
Food Shopping/Delivery Service ($25,000 / $50,000++)
Herb Farming ($10,000-$30,000 / $40,000+)
Senior Day Care ($10,000-$100,000 / $40,000++)
Licensing required.
Travel Agency ($25,000-$50,000 / $50,000+)
Appointments & expertise.
Home Inspection Service ($10,000-$20,000 / $60,000) R.E.
license helpful.
Maid Service ($1,000-$25,000 / $20,000-$40,000)
Vending Machines Routes ($10,000-$50,000 / $25,000-
$100,000)
Consignment (Used) Furniture ($20,000-$40,000 / $40,000-
$80,000)
Bed and Breakfast Inn ($50,000-$500,000 / $50,000++)
Got a house?
Crafts Shop ($10,000-$20,000 / $20,000-$50,000)
Freelance Writing ($3,000-$10,000 / $20,000-$50,000)

***Recycling People and Products:*** In this country, famed for its
largesses and excesses, its built-in obsolescence and waste, the
idea of recycling not only retired people but products that are
slated for "retirement" to a landfill or garbage dump, is both an
opportunity and a need. We have talked about "repackaging"
people for the labor market, about networking, free help from
the SBA and relation organizations, business incubators and
opportunities. And we also need to point out once more that our

global environment is crying for a thousand ways of cleaning up the air, water, soil, and a million manufactured and grown products. Such opportunities are spelled out in this writer's book, *The Green Entrepreneur* (McGraw-Hill), and Steven J. Bennett's *Ecopreneuring* (John Wiley & Sons). Recycling people means training for jobs and businesses that are either different from those in which the person was trained or that upgrade the person's skills in his/her own field, or — as organizations such as SCORE and SBDC do — prepare former employed people for entrepreneurial independence. Recycling products means giving paper, plastics, glass, wood, mineral products, and many manufactured goods a second lease on life while at the same time preventing overflow of our shrinking disposal and incineration facilities. The situation will get worse before it becomes better, and thus the opportunities for experienced entrepreneurs — particularly second careerists — is positively infinite.

*Second-Time-Around Retailing:* We feel that the continued rise of prices for goods, the forced obsolescence of products and styles, and the acceptance, especially during recession years, of buying goods that have been recycled, will enhance the increase in second-hand stores.

Of course we usually do not call these "recycled goods" shops second-hand stores. All kinds of fancy and metaphorical titles make them more attractive to customers well above the poverty level. The very popularity of *recycling,* which has assumed an almost patriotic tone, will continue to enhance the formation of stores for the re-sale, by outright purchase or consignment, of goods like children's clothing and toys, high fashions, gift ware, furniture, and jewelry.

Professionally run garage and attic sales, high-class clothing stores that offer children's and fashionable ladies' wear and are often located in prestige areas, "estate sales" of better jewelry within high-class shops or out of upper middleclass homes, book stores that offer an eclectic assortment of books and art, stores stocked with all kinds of collectibles that have long been accepted, and even toy stores that feature increasingly costly stuffed and electronic toys that privileged tots have tired of...all of these are valid retail businesses that attract retirees who like the stationary life. All of them can be low overhead, low-capitalization enterprises, since inventory can be obtained on consignment, without any cash being invested up front, other than the cost of the premises and some promotional expenses.

*Personal Services:* As our population ages, becomes more financially able and stable, as well as more indulgent, personal services will continue to grow in popularity and need. These can include maid service, party-entertainment assistance, home maintenance services, gift and reminder services, visiting health care, financial and accounting management, shopping services, transportation needs, senior day care, food preparation for both daily need and parties, learning centers to compensate for decentralized and declining public facilities, fitness and weight control plans, computer consultation and operation, and gourmet foods preparation and delivery.

No doubt there are many more, but these are the cream of the crop in opportunities for retirees re-entering the business world. Large congregate living complexes, such as Leisure World, Century Villages, the Marriott and Hyatt developments, and a hundred more, all contribute to the accessibility of such services reaching out for a concentrated market. Many of these can be organized and operated out of a home and launched with a minimum of capitalization.

Home sales party businesses can also be lumped under *personal services,* because they make it convenient for potential customers to consider purchases of jewelry, cosmetics, housewares, toys and more within the home of the "hostess" who invites a number of friends in for the pitch and pie.

## AMERICA, THE SHAPE TO COME

As the world goes, the United States is a young nation. Youth has always been venerated. Looking at the entertainment world, it appears that only the young, barely past puberty, make up an audience. Yet some in this industry are taking notice. *"Cocoon"* was an extremely popular movie about oldsters who refused to grow old. *"The Golden Girls"* and *"Murder She Wrote"* star seniors in lead roles on TV. *"Lears",* a magazine purported "for the woman who was not born yesterday", was started by Frances Lear in 1988 when she was at retirement age.

Restaurants are taking notice of the preferences of senior customers by setting aside no-smoking sections and quiet corners, and offering more salads and no-cholesterol foods. Travel is geared to that great mass of silver-tops who have the time, money, and energy to see the world. Education has discovered a major market among the post-work generation.

At Harvard's Institute for Learning in Retirement, around 400 seniors pay nearly $200 a semester for classes in continuing education — and this is one of more than 250 programs nationwide. Higher education has become a popular hobby for seniors and it will continue to proliferate.

"Many seniors," said one 72-year-old spokesperson, "...are full of zoom and boom and want to keep on learning with people their own age. I don't consider myself old. It's all in your mind."

Ken Dychtwald, author of *Age Wave* and researcher into the aging of America since 1974, predicts: "As more and more older people continue to work, business leaders will increasingly recognize the value of older workers. More and more, the overemphasis on the perceived strength and eagerness of young workers will be balanced by an appreciation for the sound judgment, personal skills, accumulated experience, low absenteeism, and ready availability of older workers."

America has focused for more than a score of years on the big baby boom generation. Well, for the record, in just a few years — 1996 to be exact — the baby boomers will turn fifty. They will see to it that the senior market will grow and continue to create opportunities for entrepreneurs.

By the year 2000, the fifty-and-older age group will grow by 18.5 percent during the 1990s — going from 64 million to 76 million people. In contrast, consuming Americans under fifty will grow by only 3.5 percent.

The psychology of marketing tells us that older customers are more comfortable with older purveyors and service people. Pharmacies, clothing retailers, financial services, health care, and restaurants — the human services rather than the high-tech industries — are the ones that will need more and more workers. And seniors who want to work can find more ready employment in these categories — usually at their own option and within their own time frames.

Isaac Asimov, the prolific writer and futurist, pointed out that the future may be brighter than we think. Sixty years ago, nobody had heard of a jet pilot, an anchor man or woman, a computer programmer or television repairman, an astronaut or a molecular biologist. In just a few more years, many people will be working at jobs of which we have not yet even heard.

Remember Betty Friedan, the firebrand women's liberationist and the author of *The Feminine Mystique?* She is 70 years old now and admits that "senior citizens are on the verge of the next great revolution...The whole thing is changing so much, I can't conceive of the ways we'll be thinking ten years from now. We will redefine the values of society and it will be a great change from this era of yuppies, when values are defined by youth."

Among the business of Volunteerism, many changes are also predicted. We mention this non-entrepreneurial activity here, because it is so part and parcel of the American fabric. We have discussed some aspects of it in Chapter IX and how volunteering can occasionally become part of entrepreneurial networking. A couple of years ago, the American Red Cross issued a report called *Volunteer 2000,* which made some important prognostications for us:

- There will be more competition for volunteers in the future, because the rate of growth of America's population is declining.

- Most population growth will take place in the South and West.

- Aging baby boomers will probably present opportunity for increased participation in volunteer activities, as they become settled in their careers and attain more free time.

- By 2000, one in three Americans will be of an ethnic or racial minority — where most of the growth will take place.

- Female participation in the labor force will continue to increase. Nearly 65% of women will be in the labor force. Working women volunteer more than non-working women, though they contribute fewer hours.

- As more people enter the workforce, fewer will be available for volunteer work, especially during working hours.

• Flexible working hours will increase, working couples will spend more time together, and volunteer organizations must accommodate themselves to this flexibility as well.

• About 45% of Americans will put in nearly five hours a week in volunteer activities.

• Most volunteering will be on a project basis, rather than long-term commitments, making it necessary for volunteer organization to develop more specific projects.

• There will be increased competition for volunteers, even though there has been and will be increased propensity for people to serve in volunteer capacities.

## INDEPENDENCE VS. BEING THE BOSS

The major portion of *second careerists* are projecting a life as independent entrepreneurs. They will have no one to depend on except themselves — with the support, of course, of their spouses and families. But many will enter full-blown businesses that demand employees. It is here that future trends need to be examined and weighed. The following trends appear evident:

• Increased wage costs

• Additional benefits, especially the kind that will attract and keep older employees

• Restructuring work practices that will appeal to the baby boomer generation — including flextime, day care, decentralized workplaces, recreation time

• Programs to increase productivity and quality consciousness.

The chief economist of the U.S. Small Business Administration, Dr. Thomas Gray, has offered a four-part approach to increased labor productivity:

1. Technology — Small business will find it difficult to compete with larger companies with larger capital. Therefore, small entrepreneurs must adopt the best available technology and integrate it fully into the production process.
2. Outside help — External technical experts, whether in technology or management, should be utilized when it is

necessary to analyze small business problems and develop appropriate solutions.

3. Training — Small business needs to increase training of the workforce, particularly after technical solutions are developed. This training should even reach into local schools that will provide newcomers to the labor pool.

4. Management — Close attention must be paid to improving management techniques. This means taking employees into confidence. They want to be consulted and to understand the thinking behind decisions. They want recognition as well as a part in the decision-making process. Enhancing day-to-day communication between the owners-managers of small business and employees improves the productivity of all small business resources.

The year 2000 is not far away and 2010 will be seen by some of us. The baby boom generation will be gray by that time and lining up for their retirement awards. How life will have changed.

Back in 1935, when a man named Franklin Delano Roosevelt announced in his radio chat (nobody had ever heard of television, with the possible exception of David Sarnoff) that from here on out and forever, all working Americans would be taken care of by a new agency called Social Security, retirement was set at 65. The average male could then expect to live another twelve years and SSA pension payments were calibrated accordingly.

And so, here it is into the '90s, and between modern medicine, nutritional science and the grim reaper, we can expect to push that average age to fifteen years beyond 65. By 2025, that figure will most likely be twenty.

Chances are that future retirement age will be elevated to 67 and deductions for earlier retirement options will be increased. We just cannot have it both ways. Our children are already burdened with paying the bill for our past excesses.

From the entrepreneurial perspective, longer life spans will mean more men and women, gray-tops and all, will opt to work longer, start new jobs, and most importantly, will start new businesses that will not only help them live better, but infuse the American economy with new vigor, taxes, and GNP.

And that's the way it will go. The American economic pendulum swings back and forth, and when it stops, it is always a little ahead. That's why this writer has faith in the United States of America and especially in its older, but too-young-to-retire, generation. And now, if you'll excuse me, I must end this book. You see, I have this great idea for another book...

# EPILOGUE

From all the foregoing information, a number of things stand out. Life is not over until you stop living. Opportunities don't stop just because you've grown gray. All trends are in our favor — education, living facilities, medical advances — and all the signs we see are on Go. In the past half century, we have contributed to many of the problems: pollution, continual deficit financing, staggering debts left to the next generation, and social aberrations that seem to have come along with us since the days of Eden. But now we realize that we can no longer borrow from the future. The future is here. We are on the leading edge of it and we have but a few years to contribute to it. That's what this book is all about: to make the very best of what we are capable of — and that is plenty. We have the knowledge, the wisdom, the experience, the money, and even the willingness to make some more contributions to our society, our families, and ourselves. There are only a few feet of difference between a rut and a grave, and we certainly don't want to hasten the latter. Being busy and productive, each in our own way and according to our own capacity, is the greatest contribution we can make — *especially* to ourselves.

## FEDERAL INFORMATION CENTERS

The Federal Information Center Program (FIC) is a one-stop source of assistance when you have a question of problem related to the Federal Government. The FIC will answer your question or assist you in finding the right office for the answer. For a more complete description of the service see Chapter 3.

Please call the number listed below for your metropolitan area or State. If your area is not listed, call (301) 722-9098 or write to Federal Information Center, P.O. Box 600, Cumberland, MD 21501-0600. Users of Telecommunications Devices for the Deaf (TDD/TTY) may call toll-free from any point in the United States by dialing (800) 326-2996.

**Alabama:**
Birmingham, Mobile                 (800) 366-2998

**Alaska:**
Anchorage                      (800) 729-8003

**Arizona:**
Phoenix                         (800) 359-3997

**Arkansas:**
Little Rock                    (800) 366-2998

**California:**
Los Angeles, San Diego
San Francisco, Santa Ana      (800) 726-4995
Sacramento                   (916) 973-1695

**Colorado:**
Colorado Springs,
Denver, Pueblo                (800) 359-3997

**Connecticut:**
Hartford, New Haven         (800) 347-1997

**Florida:**
Fort Lauderdale,
Jacksonville, Miami,
Orlando, St. Petersburg,
Tampa, West Palm Beach (800) 347-1997

**Georgia:**
Atlanta (800) 347-1997

**Hawaii:**
Honolulu (800) 733-5996

**Illinois:**
Chicago (800) 366-2998

**Indiana:**
Gary (800) 366-2998
Indianapolis (800) 347-1997

**Iowa:**
All locations (800) 735-8004

**Kansas:**
All locations (800) 735-8004

**Kentucky:**
Louisville (800) 347-1997

**Louisiana:**
New Orleans (800) 366-2998

**Maryland:**
Baltimore (800) 347-1997

**Massachusetts:**
Boston (800) 347-1997

**Michigan:**
Detroit, Grand Rapids (800) 347-1997

**Minnesota:**
Minneapolis (800) 366-2998

**Missouri:**
St. Louis (800) 366-2998
All other locations (800) 735-8004

**Nebraska:**

| | |
|---|---|
| Omaha | (800) 366-2998 |
| All other locations | (800) 735-8004 |

**New Jersey:**

| | |
|---|---|
| Newark, Trenton | (800) 735-8004 |

**New Mexico:**

| | |
|---|---|
| Albuquerque | (800) 359-1997 |

**New York:**

| | |
|---|---|
| Albany, Buffalo,<br>New York, Rochester,<br>Syracuse | (800) 347-1997 |

**North Carolina:**

| | |
|---|---|
| Charlotte | (800) 347-1997 |

**Ohio:**

| | |
|---|---|
| Akron, Columbus, Cincinnati,<br>Dayton, Cleveland, Toledo | (800) 347-1997 |

**Oklahoma:**

| | |
|---|---|
| Oklahoma City, Tulsa | (800) 366-2998 |

**Oregon:**

| | |
|---|---|
| Portland | (800) 726-4995 |

**Pennsylvania:**

| | |
|---|---|
| Philadelphia, Pittsburgh | (800) 347-1997 |

**Rhode Island:**

| | |
|---|---|
| Providence | (800) 347-1997 |

**Tennessee:**

| | |
|---|---|
| Chattanooga | (800) 347-1997 |
| Memphis, Nashville | (800) 366-2998 |

**Texas:**

| | |
|---|---|
| Austin, Dallas, Fort Worth,<br>Houston, San Antonio | (800) 366-2998 |

**Utah:**

| | |
|---|---|
| Salt Lake City | (800) 359-3997 |

**Virginia:**
  Norfolk, Richmond,
  Roanoke                                              (800) 347-1997
**Washington:**
  Seattle, Tacoma                                      (800) 726-4995
**Wisconsin:**
  Milwaukee                                            (800) 366-2998

# *Appendix 2*

## SBA Field Offices

**Alabama**
Suite 200
2121 8th Avenue N
Birmingham, AL 35203-2398
(205) 731-1344

**Alaska**
222 West 8th Avenue
Anchorage, AK 99513-7559
(907) 271-4022

**Arizona**
Suite 800
2828 N. Central Avenue
Phoenix, AZ 85004-1025
(602) 640-2316

300 W. Congress Street
Tucson, AZ 85701
(602) 629-6715

**Arkansas**
2120 Riverfront Drive
Little Rock, AR 72202
(501) 324-5278

**California**
660 J Street
Sacramento, CA 95814
(916) 551-1426

880 Front Street
San Diego, CA 92188-270
(619) 557-7252

4th Floor
211 Main Street
San Francisco, CA 94105
(415) 744-6820

20th Floor
71 Stevenson Street
San Francisco, CA 94105
(415) 774-6402

Suite 160
901 W. Civic Center Drive
Santa Ana, CA 92703
(714) 836-2494

Suite 10
6477 Telephone Road
Ventura, CA 93003
(805) 642-1866

**Colorado**
Suite 70
999 18th Street
Denver, CO 80202
(303) 294-7186

**Connecticut**
2nd Floor
330 Main Street
Hartford, CT 06106
(203) 240-4700

**District Of Columbia**
6th Floor
1111 18th Street, NW
Washington, DC 20036
(202) 634-1500

**Delaware**
Suite 412
920 N. King Street
Wilmington, DE 19801
(302) 573-6295

**Florida**
1320 S. Dixie Highway
Suite 501
Coral Gables, FL 33146
(305) 536-5521

Suite 100-B
7825 Baymeadows Way
Jacksonville, FL 32256-7504
(904) 443-1900

Suite 104
501 East Polk Street
Tampa, FL 33602-3945
(813) 228-2594

Suite 402
5601 Corporate Way
W. Palm Bch., FL 33407-2044
(407) 689-3922

**Georgia**
5th Floor
1375 Peachtree Street, NE
Atlanta, GA 30367-8102
(404) 347-2797

6th Floor
1720 Peachtree Rd., NW
Atlanta, GA 30309
(404) 347-4749

Room 225
52 N. Main Street
Statesboro, GA 30458
(912) 489-8719

**Hawaii**
300 Ala Moana Boulevard
Honolulu, HI 96850
(808) 541-2990

**Idaho**
1020 Main Street
Boise, ID 83702
(208) 334-1696

**Illinois**
Suite 1975
300 S. Riverside Plaza
Chicago, IL 60606-6617
(312) 353-0359

Room 1250
500 W. Madison Street
Chicago, IL 60661-2511
(312) 353-4528

Suite 302
511 W. Capitol Street
Springfield, IL 62704
(217) 492-4416

**Indiana**
Suite 100
429 N. Pennsylvania
Indianapolis, IN 46204-1873
(317) 226-7272

**Iowa**
Room 749
New Federal Building
210 Walnut Street
Des Moines, IA 50309
(515) 284-4422

**Kansas**
Suite 510
100 East English Street
Wichita, KS 67202
(316) 269-6273

**Kentucky**
Room 188
600 Dr. M.L.K. Jr. Pl
Louisville, KY 40202
(502) 582-5971

**Louisiana**
Suite 2000
1661 Canal Street
New Orleans, LA 70113
(504) 589-6685

**Massachusetts**
9th Floor
155 Federal Street
Boston, MA 02110
(617)451-2023

Room 265
10 Causeway Street
Boston, MA 02222-1093
(617) 565-5590

Room 212
1550 Main Street
Springfield, MA 01103
(413) 785-0268

**Maryland**
3rd Floor
10 N. Calvert Street
Baltimore, MD 21202
(410) 962-4392

**Maine**
Room 512
40 Western Avenue
Augusta, ME 04330
(207 622-8378

**Michigan**
Room 515
477 Michigan Avenue
Detroit, MI 48226
(313) 226-6075

(906) 225-1108
300 S. Front Street
Marquette, MI 49885

**Minnesota**
Suite 610
100 N. 6th Street
Minneapolis, MN 55403-1563
(612) 370-2324

**Mississippi**
Suite 1001
One Hancock Plaza
Gulfport, MS 39501-7758
(601) 863-4449

Suite 400
101 W. Capitol Street
Jackson, MS 39201
(601) 965-4378

**Missouri**
13th Floor
911 Walnut Street
Kansas City, MO 64106
(816) 426-3608

Room 242
815 Olive Street
St. Louis, MO 63101
(314) 539-6600

**Montana**
Room 528
301 S. Park
Helena, MT 59626
(406) 449-5381

**Nebraska**
11145 Mill Valley Road
Omaha, NE 68154
(402) 221-4691

**Nevada**
Room 301
301 E. Stewart Street
Las Vegas, NV 89125-2527
(702) 388-6611

**North Carolina**
200 N. College Street
Charlotte, NC 28202
(704) 344-6563

**North Dakota**
Room 218
Federal Building
657 2nd Avenue, North
Fargo, ND 58108-3086
(701) 239-5131

**New Hampshire**
Suite 202
143 N. Main Street
Concord, NH O3302-1257
(603) 225-1400

**New Jersey**
2600 Mt. Ephrain Ave
Camden, NJ 08104
(609) 757-5183

4th Floor
60 Park Place
Newark, NJ 07102
(201) 645-2434

**New Mexico**
625 Silver SW
Albuquerque, NM 87102
(505) 766-1870

**New York**
Room 222
445 Broadway
Albany, NY 12207
(518) 472-6300

Room 1311
111 W. Huron Street
Buffalo, NY 14202
(716) 846-4301

4th Floor
333 E. Water Street
Elmira, NY 14901
(607) 734-8130

Room 102E
35 Pinelawn Road
Melville, NY 11747
(516) 454-0750

Room 31-08
26 Federal Plaza
New York, NY 10278
(212) 264-1450

Room 3100
26 Federal Plaza
New York, NY 10278
(212) 264-2454

Room 410
100 State Street
Rochester, NY 14614
(716) 263-6700

Room 1071
100 S. Clinton Street
Syracuse, NY 13260
(315) 423-5383

**Ohio**
Suite 870
525 Vine Street
Cincinnati, OH 45202
(513) 684-2814

Room 317
1240 E. 9th Street
Cleveland, OH 44199
(216) 522-4180

Suite 1400
2 Nationwide Plaza
Columbus, OH 43215
(614) 469-6860

**Oklahoma**
Suite 670
200 N.W. 5th Street
Oklahoma City, OK 73102
(405) 231-4301

**Oregon**
Suite 500
222 S.W. Columbia
Portland, OR 97201
(503) 326-2682

**Pacific Islands**
20th Floor
71 Stevenson Street
San Francisco, CA 94105
(415) 774-6402

**Pennsylvania**
Room 309
100 Chestnut Street
Harrisburg, PA 17101
(717) 782-3840

Suite 201
475 Allendale Road
King Prussia, PA 19406
(215) 962-3700

5th Floor
960 Penn Avenue
Pittsburgh, PA 15222
(412) 644-2780

Room 2327
20 N. Pennsylvania Avenue
Wilkes-Barre, PA 18702
(717) 826-6497

**Puerto Rico**
Room 691
Carlos Chardon Avenue
Hato Rey, PR 00918
(809) 766-5572

**Rhode Island**
5th Floor
380 Westminster Mall
Providence, RI 02903
(401) 528-4561

**South Carolina**
Room 358
1835 Assembly Street
Columbia, SC 29201
(803) 765-5376

**South Dakota**
Suite 101
101 South Main Avenue
Sioux Falls, SD 57102-0527
(605) 330-4231

**Tennessee**
Suite 201
50 Vantage Way
Nashville, TN 37228-1500
(615) 736-5881

**Texas**
Suite 1200
606 N. Carancanua
Corpus Christi, TX 78476
(512) 888-3331

Building C
8625 King George Drive
Dallas, TX 75235-3391
(214) 767-7633

Room 3C-36
1100 Commerce Street
Dallas, TX 75242
(214) 767-0605

Suite 320
10737 Gateway W.
El Paso, TX 79935
(915) 540-5676

9301 SW Freeway Suite 550
Houston, TX 77074-1591
(713) 953-5900

Room 500
222 East Van Buren Street
Harlingen, TX 78550
(512) 427-8533

Room 200
1611 Tenth Street
Lubbock, TX 79401
(806) 743-7462

Room 103
505 E. Travis
Marshall, TX 75670
(903) 935-5257

Suite 200
7400 Blanco Road
San Antonio, TX 78216
(512) 229-4535

**Utah**
Room 2237
Federal Building
125 South State Street
Salt Lake City, UT 84138-1195
(801) 524-5800

**Virginia**
Room 3015
400 N. 8th Street
Richmond, VA 23240
(804) 771-2400

**Virgin Islands**
Suite 7
4200 United Shopping Plaza
St. Croix, VI 00820
(809) 778-5380

Room 210
Veterans Drive
St. Thomas, VI 00802
(809) 774-8530

**Vermont**
Room 205
87 State Street
Montpelier, VT 05602
(802) 828-4422

**Washington**
10th Floor E
W. 601 First Avenue
Spokane, WA 99204-0317
(509) 353-2800

**Wisconsin**
Room 213
212 E. Washington Avenue
Madison, WI 53703
(608) 264-5261

Suite 400
310 W. Wisconsin Avenue
Milwaukee, WI 53203
(414) 297-3941

**West Virginia**
Room 309
550 Eagan Street
Charleston, WV 25301
(304) 347-5220

5th Floor
168 W. Main Street
Clarksburg, WV 26301
(304) 623-5631

**Wyoming**
Room 4001
Federal Building
100 East B Street
999 18th Street
Casper, WY 82602-2839
(307) 261-5761

# APPENDIX 3

## SMALL BUSINESS DEVELOPMENT CENTERS

S BDCs are supported by SBA annually in 49 states for $50 million. SBDC's offer "one stop" assistance to small businesses, making a variety of information and guidance available on management techniques and technology. Most SBDCs are headquartered at one of the 56 "lead" universities or colleges with nearly 600 subcenters located through the U.S. in easily accessible locations.

**ALABAMA**
Ms. Pat Thompson
Acting State Director
Small Business Development Center
University of Alabama in Birmingham
17178 11th Avenue South, Suite 419    (205) 934-7260
Birmingham, AL 35294    (205) 934-7645 FAX

**ALASKA**
Ms. Jan Fredericks
State Director
Small Business Development Center
University of Alaska/Anchorage
430 West 7th Avenue, Suite 115    (907) 274-7232
Anchorage, AK 99501    (907) 274-9524 FAX

**ARIZONA**
Mr. Dave Smith
State Director
Small Business Development Center
Gateway Community College
108 North 40th Street, Suite 148    (602) 392-5224
Phoenix, AZ 85034    (602) 392-5300 FAX

## ARKANSAS
Mr. Paul McGinnis
State Director
Small Business Development Center
University of Arkansas
Little Rock Technology Center
100 South Main, Suite 401                     (501) 324-9043
Little Rock, AR 72201                          (501) 324-9049 FAX

## CALIFORNIA
Dr. Edward Kawahara
State Director
Small Business Development Center
Department of Commerce
801 K Street, Suite 1600
Sacramento, CA 95814                          (916) 324-9234

## COLORADO
Mr. Rick Garcia
State Director
Small Business Development Center
Office of Business Development
1625 Broadway, Suite 1710                     (303) 892-3840
Denver, CO 80203                               (303) 892-3848 FAX

## CONNECTICUT
Mr. John P. O'Conner
State Director
Small Business Development Center
University of Connecticut
Box U-41, Room. 422
368 Fairfield Road                             (203) 486-4135
Storrs, CT 06268                               (203) 486-1576 FAX

## DELAWARE
Ms. Linda Fayerweather
State Director
Small Business Development Center
University of Delaware
Suite 005 - Purnell Hall                       (302) 451-2747
Newark, DE 19711                               (302) 451-6750 FAX

## DISTRICT OF COLUMBIA
Ms. Nancy A. Flake
State Director
Small Business Development Center
Howard University
2600 6th Street, NW                                  (202) 806-1550
Washington, DC 20059                              (202) 806-1777 FAX

## FLORIDA
Mr. Jerry Cartwright
State Director
Small Business Development Center
University of West Florida
11000 University Parkway                             (904) 474-3016
Pensacola, FL 32514                              (904) 474-2030 FAX

## GEORGIA
Mr. Hank Logan
State Director
Small Business Development Center
University of Georgia
Chicopee Complex                                     (404) 542-5760
Athens, GA 30602                                 (404) 542-6776 FAX

## HAWAII
Ms. Janet Nye
State Director
Small Business Development Center
University of Hawaii at Hilo
523 West Lanikaula Street                            (808) 933-3515
Hilo, HI 96720-4091                              (808) 933-3622 FAX

## IDAHO
Mr. Ronald R. Hall
State Director
Small Business Development Center
Boise State University
College of Business
1910 University Drive                                (208) 385-1640
Boise, ID 83725                                  (208) 385-3877 FAX

## ILLINOIS

Mr. Jeffrey J. Mitchell
State Director
Small Business Development Center
Department of Commerce and Community Affairs
620 East Adams Street                          (217) 524-5856
Springfield, IL 62701                      (217) 785-6328 FAX

## INDIANA

Mr. Steve Thrash
State Director
Small Business Development Center
Economic Development Council
One North Capitol, Suite 420                   (317) 264-6871
Indianapolis, IN 46204-2248                (317) 264-3102 FAX

## IOWA

Mr. Ronald Manning
State Director
Small Business Development Center
Iowa State University
137 Lynn Avenue                                (515) 292-6351
Ames, IA 50010                             (515) 292-0020 FAX

## KANSAS

Mr. Tom Hull
State Director
Small Business Development Center
Wichita State University
Campus Box 148                                 (316) 689-3193
Wichita, KS 67208-1595                     (316) 689-3647 FAX

## KENTUCKY

Ms. Janet Holloway
State Director
Small Business Development Center
University of Kentucky
College of Business and Economics
205 Business & Economics Building              (606) 257-7668
Lexington, KY 40506-00341                  (606) 258-1907 FAX

## LOUISIANA
Dr. John Baker
State Director
Small Business Development Center
Northeast Louisiana University
College of Business Administration
700 University Avenue (318) 342-5506
Monroe, LA 71209 (318) 342-5510 FAX

## MAINE
Ms. Diane Branscomb
Acting State Director
Small Business Development Center
University of Southern Maine
15 Surrenden Street (207) 780-4420
Portland, ME 04101 (207) 780-4417 FAX

## MARYLAND
Mr. Michael E. Long, Jr.
Acting State Director
Small Business Development Center
Department of Economic and Employment Development
217 East Redwood Street, 10th Floor (301) 333-6996
Baltimore, MD 21202 (301) 333-6608 FAX

## MASSACHUSETTS
Mr. John Ciccarelli
State Director
Small Business Development Center
University of Massachusetts
School of Management (413) 545-6301
Amherst, MA 01003 (413) 545-1273 FAX

## MICHIGAN
Dr. Norman Schlafmann
State Director
Small Business Development Center
Wayne State University
2727 Second Avenue (313) 577-4848
Detroit, MI 48201 (313) 577-4222 FAX

**MINNESOTA**
Randall Olson
State Director
Small Business Development Center
Department of Trade and Economic Development
American Center Building
150 East Kellogg Boulevard                      (612) 297-5773
St. Paul, MN 55101-1421                          (612) 296-1290 FAX

**MISSISSIPPI**
Mr. Raleigh Byars
State Director
Small Business Development Center
University of Mississippi
Old Chemistry Building, Suite 216               (601) 232-5001
University, MS 38677                             (601) 232-7010 FAX

**MISSOURI**
Mr. Max E. Summers
State Director
Small Business Development Center
University of Missouri
Suite 300, University Place                     (314) 882-1348
Columbia, MO 65211                              (314) 884-4297 FAX

**MONTANA**
Mr. Evan McKinney
Acting State Director
Small Business Development Center
Department of Commerce
1424 Ninth Avenue                               (406) 444-4780
Helena, MT 59620                                (406) 444-2808 FAX

**NEBRASKA**
Mr. Robert Bernie
State Director
Small Business Development Center
University of Nebraska at Omaha
Peter Kiewit Center                             (402) 554-2521
Omaha, NE 68182                                 (402) 595-2388 FAX

**NEVADA**
Mr. Samuel Males
State Director
Small Business Development Center
University of Nevada in Reno
College of Business Administration,
Room 411 (702) 784-1717
Reno, NV 89557-0016 (702) 784-4305 FAX

**NEW HAMPSHIRE**
Ms. Helen Goodman
State Director
Small Business Development Center
University of New Hampshire
108 McConnell Hall (603) 862-2200
Durham, NH 03824 (603) 862-4468 FAX

**NEW JERSEY**
Ms. Brenda B. Hopper
State Director
Small Business Development Center
Rutgers University
Ackerson Hall - 3rd Floor
180 University Street (201) 648-5950
Newark, NJ 07102 (201) 648-1110 FAX

**NEW MEXICO**
Mr. Randy Grissom
State Director
Small Business Development Center
Santa Fe Community College
P.O. Box 4187
Santa Fe, NM 87502-4187 (505) 438-1237 FAX

**NEW YORK**
Mr. James L. King
State Director
Small Business Development Center
State University of New York
SUNY Upstate
SUNY Plaza, S-523 (518) 443-5398
Albany, NY 12246 (518) 465-4992 FAX

Dr. Solomon S. Kabuka, Jr.
Director
Small Business Development Center
University of The Virgin Islands
Grand Hotel Building, Annex B
P.O. Box 1087                                          (809) 776-3206
St. Thomas, U.S. Virgin Islands 00804   (809) 775-3756 FAX

**NORTH CAROLINA**
Mr. Scott Daugherty
State Director
Small Business Development Center
University of North Carolina
4509 Creedmoor Road, Suite 201                        (919) 571-4154
Raleigh, NC 27612                                 (919) 787-9284 FAX

**NORTH DAKOTA**
Mr. Wally Kearns
State Director
Small Business Development Center
University of North Dakota
Gamble Hall, University Station                       (701) 777-3700
Grand Forks, ND 58202-7308                       (701) 223-3081 FAX

**OHIO**
Mr. Jack Brown
State Director
Small Business Development Center
Department of Development
30 East Broad Street
Columbus, OH 43266-1001                               (614) 466-5111

**OKLAHOMA**
Dr. Grady Pennington
State Director
Small Business Development Center
Southeast Oklahoma State University
517 West University
Station A, Box 2584                                    (405) 924-0277
Durant, OK 74701                                  (405) 924-8531 FAX

## OREGON
Mr. Sandy Cutler
State Director
Small Business Development Center
Lane Community College
99 West 10th Avenue, Suite 216            (503) 726-2250
Eugene, OR 97401                          (503) 345-6006 FAX

## PENNSYLVANIA
Mr. Gregory L. Higgins
State Director
Small Business Development Center
University of Pennsylvania
The Wharton School
444 Vance Hall                            (215) 898-1219
Philadelphia, PA 19104                    (215) 898-1299 FAX

## PUERTO RICO
Mr. Jose M. Romaguera
Director
Small Business Development Center
University of Puerto Rico
Box 5253 - College Station
Building B
Mayaguez, PR 00708            (809) 834-3590 or 834-3790

## RHODE ISLAND
Mr. Douglas Jobling
State Director
Small Business Development Center
Bryant College
1150 Douglas Pike                         (401) 232-6111
Smithfield, RI 02917-1284                 (401) 232-6319 FAX

## SOUTH CAROLINA
Mr. John Lenti
State Director
Small Business Development Center
University of South Carolina
College of Business Administration
1710 College Street                          (803) 777-4907
Columbia, SC 29208                           (803) 777-4403 FAX

## SOUTH DAKOTA
M. Donald Greenfield
State Director
Small Business Development Center
University of South Dakota
School of Business
414 East Clark                               (605) 677-5272
Vermilion, SD 57069                          (605) 677-5427 FAX

## TENNESSEE
Dr. Kenneth J. Burns
State Director
Small Business Development Center
Memphis State University                     (901) 678-2500
Memphis, TN 38152                            (901) 678-4072 FAX

## TEXAS
Dr. Elizabeth Gatewood
Region Director
Small Business Development Center
University of Houston
601 Jefferson, Suite 2330                    (713) 752-8444
Houston, TX 77002                            (713) 752-8484 FAX

Mr. Robert M. McKinley
Region Director
South Texas-Border
Small Business Development Center
University of Texas at San Antonio           (512) 224-0791
San Antonio, TX 78285-0660                   (512) 222-9834 FAX

Mr. Craig Bean
Acting Region Director
Northwest Texas
Small Business Development Center
Texas Tech University
2579 South Loop 289, Suite 114 (806) 745-3973
Lubbock, TX 79423-1637 (806) 745-6207 FAX

Ms. Marty Jones
Region Director
North Texas
Small Business Development Center
Dallas Community College
1402 Corinth Street (214) 565-5831
Dallas, TX 75215 (214) 324-7945 FAX

**UTAH**
Mr. David Nimkin
State Director
Small Business Development Center
University of Utah
102 West 500 South (801) 581-7905
Salt Lake City, UT 84102 (801) 581-7814 FAX

**VERMONT**
Mr. Norris Elliott
State Director
Small Business Development Center
University of Vermont
Extension Service
Morrill Hall (802) 656-4479
Burlington, VT 05405 (802) 656-8642 FAX

**VIRGINIA**
Dr. Robert Smith
State Director
Small Business Development Center
Department of Economic Development
1021 East Cary Street (804) 8258
Richmond, VA 23219-798 (804) 371-8185 FAX

**WASHINGTON**
Mr. Lyle M. Anderson
State Director
Small Business Development Center
Washington State University
College of Business and Economics          (509) 335-1576
Pullman, WA 99164                          (509) 335-0949 FAX

**WEST VIRGINIA**
Ms. Eloise Jack
State Director
Small Business Development Center
Governor's Office of Community And Industrial
Development
1115 Virginia Street, East                 (304) 348-2960
Charleston, WV 25310                       (304) 348-0127 FAX

**WISCONSIN**
Mr. William H. Pinkovitz
State Director
Small Business Development Center
University of Wisconsin
432 North Lake Street, Room 423            (608) 263-7794
Madison, WI 53706                          (608) 262-3878 FAX

**WYOMING**
Ms. Barbara Crews
Acting State Director
Small Business Development Center
Casper Community College
111 West Second Street
Suite 416                                  (307) 235-4825
Casper, WY 82601                           (307) 473-7243 FAX

# APPENDIX 4

## GOVERNMENT PRINTING OFFICE BOOKSTORES

A free catalog of all current books, manuals, maps, and artifacts published by the Superintendent of Documents is available from the U.S. Government Printing Office, Washington, DC 20402, phone (202) 783-3238 or from any of the government bookstores. These items may also be purchased with cash or credit card at any of the following locations:

**Alabama**
O'Neill Building
2021 Third Avenue N
Birmingham, AL 35203
(205) 731-1056

**California**
ARCO Plaza, C-Level
505 Flower Street
Los Angeles, CA 90071
(213) 894-5841

Room 1023, Federal Building
450 Golden Gate Avenue
San Francisco, CA 94102
(415) 556-0643

**Colorado**
Room 117, Federal Building
1961 Stout Street
Denver, CO 80294
(303) 844-3964

World Savings Building
720 N. Main Street
Pueblo, CO 81003
(719) 544-3142

**District of Colombia**
U.S. Government
Printing Office
710 North Capital Street, NW
Washington, DC 20401
(202) 275-2091

1510 H. Street, NW
Washington, DC 20005
(202) 653-5075

**Florida**
Room 158, Federal Building
400 W. Bay Street
Jacksonville, FL 32202
(904) 791-3801

**Georgia**
Room 100, Federal Building
275 Peachtree Street NE
Atlanta, GA 30343
(404) 331-6947

**Illinois**
Room 1365, Federal Building
219 S. Dearborn Street
Chicago, IL 60604
(312) 353-5133

**Maryland**
Warehouse Sales Outlet
8660 Cherry Lane
Laurel, MD 20707
(301) 953-7974, 792-0262

**Massachusetts**
Room 179
Thomas P. O'Neill Building
10 Causeway Street
Boston, MA 02222
(617) 565-6680

**Michigan**
Suite 160, Federal Building
477 Michigan Avenue
Detroit, MI 48226
(313) 226-7816

**Missouri**
120 Bannister Mall
5600 E. Bannister Rd.
Kansas City, MO 64137
(816) 765-2256

**New York**
Room 110
26 Federal Plaza
New York, NY 10278
(212) 264-3825

**Ohio**
Room 1653, Federal Building
1240 E. 9th Street
Cleveland, OH 44199
(216) 522-4922

Room 207, Federal Building
200 N. High Street
Columbus, OH 43215
(614) 469-6956

**Oregon**
1305 S.W. First Avenue
Portland, OR 97201-5801
(503) 221-6217

**Pennsylvania**
Robert Morris Building
100 N. 17th Street
Philadelphia, PA 19103
(215) 597-0677

Room 118, Federal Building
1000 Liberty Avenue
Pittsburgh, PA 15222
(412) 644-2721

**Texas**
Room 1C46, Federal Building
1100 Commerce Street
Dallas, TX 75242
(214) 767-0076

Suite 12, Texas Crude Building
801 Travis Street
Houston, TX 77002
(713) 653-3100

**Washington**
Room 194, Federal Building
915 Second Avenue
Seattle, WA 98174
(206) 442-4270

**Wisconsin**
Room 190, Federal Building
517 E. Wisconsin Avenue
Milwaukee, WI 53202
(414) 297-1304

# APPENDIX 5

## GENERAL SERVICES ADMINISTRATION
## BUSINESS SERVICE CENTERS

*REGION*  *REGIONAL OFFICE CONTACTS*

2ADB-1  *DIRECTOR*
Tom Pendleton
*PHONE:*  (617) 565-8100
*FTS:*  835-8100
*FAX:*  565-5720
*MAILING ADDRESS*
General Services Administration
Business Service Center
Thomas P. O'Neill Federal Bldg.
10 Causeway Street, Room 290
Boston, MA 02222
*AREAS SERVICED*
Connecticut, Maine, Vermont, New Hampshire,
Massachusetts and Rhode Island

2ADB  *DIRECTOR*
Gwen Williams, Manager
*PHONE:*  (212) 264-1234
*FTS:*  264-1234
*FAX:*  264-2760
*MAILING ADDRESS*
General Services Administration
Business Service Center
Jacob K. Javits Federal Bldg.
26 Federal Plaza
New York, NY 10278
*AREAS SERVICED*
New Jersey, New York, Puerto Rico and
Virgin Islands

3ADB   *DIRECTOR*
       John Thompson
       Office of Business and Public Affairs
       *PHONE:*                            (215) 597-9613
       FTS:                                597-9613
       FAX:                                597-1122
       *MAILING ADDRESS*
       General Services Administration
       Business Service Center
       9th & Market Streets
       Philadelphia, PA 19107
       *AREAS SERVICED*
       Pennsylvania, Delaware, West Virginia Maryland
       and Virginia

4ADB   *DIRECTOR*
       Larry Fountain
       *PHONE:*                            (404) 331-5103
       FTS:                                841-5103
       FAX:                                841-5103
       *MAILING ADDRESS*
       General Services Administration
       Business Service Center
       401 West Peachtree Street
       Room 2900
       Atlanta, GA 30365-2550
       *AREAS SERVICED*
       Alabama, Florida, Kentucky, Georgia, Mississippi,
       North Carolina, South Carolina and Tennessee

5ADB   *DIRECTOR*
       James S. Czysz
       *PHONE:*                            (312) 353-5383
       FTS:                                353-5383
       FAX:                                886-9893

*MAILING ADDRESS*
General Services Administration
Business Service Center
230 South Dearborn Street
Chicago, IL 60604
*AREAS SERVICED*
Illinois, Indiana, Ohio, Michigan, Minnesota
and Wisconsin

6ADB     *DIRECTOR*
Pat Brown-Dixon
*PHONE:*                 (816) 926-7203
*FTS:*                    926-7203
*FAX:*                  926-7513
*MAILING ADDRESS*
General Services Administration
Business Service Center
1500 East Bannister Road
Kansas City, MO 64131
*AREAS SERVICED*
Iowa, Kansas, Missouri and Nebraska

7ADB     *DIRECTOR*
Dennis C. Armon
*PHONE:*                 (817) 334-3284
FTS·                    334-3284
*FAX:*                  334-4867
*MAILING ADDRESS*
General Services Administration
Business Service Center
819 Taylor Street
Fort Worth, TX 76102
*AREAS SERVICED*
Arkansas, Louisiana, Texas, New Mexico
and Oklahoma

8ADB-8  *DIRECTOR*
Darlene Kendrick
*PHONE:*                                    (303) 236-7408
FTS:                                        776-7408
FAX:                                        236-0455
FAX:                                        776-0455
*MAILING ADDRESS*
General Services Administration
Business Service Center
B41 Room 141
Denver Federal Center
Denver, CO 80225
*AREAS SERVICED*
Colorado, North Dakota, South Dakota, Utah,
Wyoming and Montana

9-ADB-S  *DIRECTOR*
Gerald D. Meckler
*PHONE:*                                    (415) 744-5050
FAX:                                        484-5068
*MAILING ADDRESS*
General Services Administration
Business Service Center
525 Market Street
San Francisco, CA 94105
*AREAS SERVICED*
Northern California, Hawaii and all of Nevada,
except Clark County

9-ADB-L  *DIRECTOR*
Carol Honore
*PHONE:*                                    (213) 894-3210
FTS:                                        798-3210
*MAILING ADDRESS*
General Services Administration
Business Service Center
300 North Los Angeles Street
Los Angeles, CA 90012-2000

AREAS SERVICED
Los Angeles, Southern California, Arizona and
Clark County, Nevada

9ADB-10 DIRECTOR
Wiletta F. Brown
PHONE:                                    (206) 931-7956
FTS:                                      396-7957
FAX:                                      396-7507
MAILING ADDRESS
General Services Administration
Business Service Center
15th & C Streets, SW
Auburn, WA 98001
AREAS SERVICED
Alaska, Idaho, Oregon and Washington

WADB    DIRECTOR
Diane Ross
Office of Business and Public Affairs
PHONE:                                    (202) 708-5804
FAX:                                      708-6420
MAILING ADDRESS
General Services Administration
Business Service Center
7th & D Streets, SW
Washington, DC 20407
AREAS SERVICED
*District of Columbia, nearby Maryland and Virginia

*Consists of District of Columbia, the counties of Montgomery
and Prince George's in Maryland, and the City of Alexandria
and the counties of Arlington, Fairfax, Loudon and Prince
William of Virginia.

## QUICK REFERENCE FEDERAL CONTACTS

| | |
|---|---|
| Agricultural Marketing Service, USDA | (202) 447-8998 |
| Animal Care, APHIS/USDA | (301) 436-7799 |
| Antitrust Division, USDOJ | (202) 633-3543 |
| Aquaculture Information Center | (301) 344-3704 |
| Bureau of Indian Affairs, DOI | (202) 343-4576 |
| Capitol, U.S. | (202) 225-6827 |
| Census Bureau, USDOC | (301) 763-4100 |
| Commodity Futures Trading Commission | (202) 254-8630 |
| Congressional Record, GPO, Subscriptions | (202) 783-3238 |
| Congressional Record Index, unpublished | (202) 275-9009 |
| Congressional Research Service | (202) 707-5700 |
| Consumer Product Safety Commission | (800) 638-2772 |
| Cooperative Extension Service, USDA | (202) 447-3029 |
| Copyrights Information, Library of Congress | (202) 479-0700 |
| Application Forms Request | (202) 707-9100 |
| Customs Service, Treasury Department | (800) 872-3253 |
| Economic Development Administration, USDOC | (202) 377-4085 |
| Education, DOE, Financial Aid Information | |
| Bilingual Clearinghouse | (800) 336-4560 |
| Energy Inquiry and Referral | (800) 523-2929 |
| Appropriate Technology Assistance | (800) 428-2525 |
| EPA Chemical Emergency Preparedness | (800) 535-0202 |
| RCRA Superfund Hotline | (800) 424-9346 |
| Pesticides Telecommunications Network | (800) 858-7378 |
| Small Business Hotline | (800) 368-5888 |
| Radon/Asbestos Hotline | (800) 334-8571 |
| Export/Import Bank | (800) 424-5201 |
| Farm Credit Administration | (703)883-4251 |
| Farmers Home Administration, USDA | (202) 475-4100 |
| Federal Communications Commission, | |
| Common Carrier/Mass Media Bureau, | |
| Small Business Assistance | (202) 632-7000 |

| | |
|---|---|
| Federal Crime Insurance | (800) 638-8780 |
| Federal Deposit Insurance Corp. | (800) 424-5488 |
| Federal Election Commission | (800) 424-9530 |
| Federal Emergency Management Agency | (800) 838-8820 |
| Federal Home Loan Bank Board | (800) 424-5404 |
| Federal Information Center, GSA | (800) 347-1997 |
| Federal Highway Administration, USDOT | (202) 366-4853 |
| Federal Register (Nat'l Archives), GPO | (202) 783-3238 |
| Statutes Unit | (202) 523-6641 |
| Public Laws Update Service (PLUS) | (202) 523-6641 |
| Flood Insurance Program, FEMA | (800) 638-6620 |
| Food & Nutrition Service, USDA | (703) 756-3276 |
| Forest Service, USDA | (404) 347-4177 |
| Garment Registration Number, FTC | (202) 326-3034 |
| General Accounting Office, Documents | (202) 275-6241 |
| General Services Administration, | |
| Small Business Service Centers | (404) 331-5103 |
| Government Printing Office, Publications | (202) 783-3238 |
| Housing & Urban Development, USHUD | (202) 755-6950 |
| Immigration & Naturalization Service, USDOJ | (800) 777-7700 |
| Internal Revenue Service, Treasury Department | (800) 829-1040 |
| | (800) 829-3676 |
| Labor/Management Standards, USDOL | (202) 523-7343 |
| Labor Surplus Areas, USDOL | (202) 535-0189 |
| Library of Congress | (202) 707-5000 |
| Meat & Poultry Inspection, FSIS/USDA | (800) 535-4555 |
| Metric Conversion Program, USDOC | (202) 377-0944 |
| National Archives | (202) 501-5000 |
| National Credit Union Administration | (202) 682-9600 |
| National Institutes of Health, | |
| Office of Technology Transfer | (301) 496-0750 |
| National Labor Relations Board | (202) 254-9430 |
| National Marine Fishery Service, | |
| USDOC/NOAA/NMFS | |
| Seafood Inspection Service | (301) 427-2355 |
| National Technical Information Service, USDOC | (800) 336-4700 |
| Oil & Chemical Spills, Natl. Response Center, | |
| USCG/USDOT | (800) 424-8802 |
| Overseas Private Investment Corp. | (800) 424-6742 |

| | |
|---|---|
| Passport Services, USDOS | (202) 647-2424 |
| Patent & Trademark Office, USDOC, | (703) 557-3341 |
| Pension Planning, IRS, SEPs #590 | (202) 566-6783 |
| Pension/Welfare Benefits Admin., USDOL | (202) 523-8921 |
| Southeastern Regional Educational Improvement | |
|   Laboratory, USDOE, | (919) 549-8216 |
| Resolution Trust Corporation, | |
|   Contractor Registration Office | (800) 541-1782 |
| Rural Information Center, | |
|   National Agricultural Library | |
|   & the Cooperative Extension Service, | (301) 344-5414 |
| Security & Exchange Commission - Filings | (202) 272-7450 |
| SBA Answer Desk, | (800) 827-5722 |
| Smithsonian Institute | (202) 357-2700 |
| Social Security Administration | (800) 772-1213 |
| U.S. Postal Service | (202) 268-2000 |
| Veterans Affairs | (202) 376-6996 |
| Visa Services, USDOS | (202) 647-0510 |
| White House, 1600 Pennsylvania Avenue, | (202) 456-7041 |
| Women's Economic Development Corps. | (800) 222-2933 |
| Weather Service, USDOC | (301) 427-7258 |
| Weights & Measures, National Institute of Standards | |
|   & Technology (NIST) USDOC, | (301) 975-4004 |

HOTLINES: The NIST maintains these hotlines with recorded messages which give weekly updates for international businesses.

| | |
|---|---|
| GATT HOTLINE | (301) 975-4041 |
| EC-92 HOTLINE | (301) 921-4164 |

# INDEX

# THE BUSINESS BOOKSHELF

These books have been carefully selected as the best on these subjects. Your satisfaction is guaranteed or your money back.

To order, call toll-free (800) 255-5730 extension 110. Please have your Visa, Mastercard, American Express or Discover card ready.

### Money Sources for Small Business
*How You Can Find Private, State, Federal, and Corporate Financing*
By William Alarid. Many potential successful business owners simply don't have enough cash to get started. *Money Sources* shows how to get money from Federal, State, Venture Capital Clubs, Corporations, Computerized Matching Services, Small Business Investment Companies plus many other sources. Includes samples of loan applications.
ISBN 0-940673-51-7    224 pages    8 1/2 x 11    paperbound    $19.95
*See special offer on last page!*

### Small Time Operator
*How to Start Your Own Business, Keep Your Books, Pay Your Taxes, and Stay Out of Trouble*
By Bernard Kamaroff, C.P.A. The most popular small business book in the U.S., it's used by over 250,000 businesses. Easy to read and use, *Small Time Operator* is particularly good for those without bookkeeping experience. Comes complete with a year's supply of ledgers and worksheets designed especially for small businesses, and contains invaluable information on permits, licenses, financing, loans, insurance, bank accounts, etc.
ISBN 0-917510-06-2    190 pages    8 1/2 x 11    paperbound    $12.95

**Puma Publishing • 1670 Coral Drive, Suite R
Santa Maria, California 93454**

## The Business Planning Guide
*Creating a Plan for Success in Your Own Business*
By Andy Bangs. *The Business Planning Guide* has been used by hundreds of banks, colleges, and accounting firms to guide business owners through the process of putting together a complete and effective business plan and financing proposal. The *Guide* comes complete with examples, forms and worksheets that make the planning process painless. With over 150,000 copies in print, the *Guide* has become a small business classic.
**ISBN 0-936894-10-5    149 pages    8 1/2 x 11    paperbound    $18.95**

## Free Help from Uncle Sam to Start Your Own Business
*(Or Expand the One You Have)* 3rd Edition
By William Alarid and Gustav Berle. *Free Help* describes over 100 government programs that help small business and give dozens of examples of how others have used this aid. Included are appendices with helpful books, organizations and phone numbers.
**ISBN 0-940673-54-1    304 pages    5 1/2 x 8 1/2    paperbound    $13.95**

## Marketing Without Advertising
By Michael Phillips and Salli Rasberry. A creative and practical guide that shows small business people how to avoid wasting money on advertising. The authors, experienced business consultants, show how to implement an ongoing marketing plan to tell potential and current customers that yours is a quality business worth trusting, recommending, and coming back to.
**ISBN 0-87337-019-8    200 pages    8 1/2 x 11    paperbound    $13.95**

## The Partnership Book
By attorneys Dennis Clifford and Ralph Warner. When two or more people join to start a small business, one of the most basic needs is to establish a solid, legal partnership agreement. This book supplies a number of sample agreements which you can use as is. Buy-out clauses, unequal sharing of assets, and limited partnerships are all discussed in detail.
**ISBN 0-87337-141-0    221 pages    8 1/2 x 11    paperbound    $24.95**

## Call Toll-Free (800) 255-5730 extension 110.
Please have Visa, Mastercard, American Express or Discover card ready, or write: Puma Publishing, 1670 Coral Drive, Suite R, Santa Maria, California 93454.
Sales Tax: Please add 7 3/4% for shipping to California addresses.
Shipping $2.00 per book; airmail $4.00 per book.

SOUTHEASTERN COMMUNITY COLLEGE LIBRARY

3 3255 00034 0480